De you

I hope ... joy it!
well and that y...
I look forward to working
together!

A very Happy New Year & all
to you! Cheers to making
our dreams come true!

Sabrina Perrot.

Mahina Perrot

WRITE & PUBLISH YOUR FIRST BOOK IN 90 DAYS

© Mahina/Maïna Perrot

The moral right of Maïna Perrot to be identified as the authors of this work has been asserted in accordance with the Copyright, Designs and Patents Act, 1988. All rights reserved.

No part of this publication may be reproduced or transmitted in any form or by any means, electronic or mechanical, including photocopy, recording, or any information storage and retrieval system, without permission in writing from the publisher.

ISBN : 9798787292220

Table of content

Introduction

"The book in you"

Why you should definitely write it

Traditional vs Vanity Publishing

Why self-publishing is the best

About me

The 12-step process

Step 1: Choose

Step 2: Research

Step 3: Plan

Step 4: Imagine

Step 5: Write

Step 6: Focus

Step 7: Flow

Step 8: Edit

Step 9: Feedback

Step 10: Design

Step 11: Publish

Step 12: Market

Conclusion

About the author

Introduction

I believe that everyone has a story to tell and that everyone's story is worth telling! I work with people who already know exactly what book they want to write but cannot conceive it being finished or completed, let alone published.

I am thrilled and proud to say that I've helped many people make their dreams of publishing their books come true. It is very fulfilling work not just for them, but for me too!

It is my wish that anyone who "has a book in them" and that is simply waiting to be born finds the strength to do it. Writing a book is a monumental task, don't get me wrong, but it is most definitely something most people can achieve, especially with some guidance!

And that is also probably the main reason why you should pick up this book.

You know you want to write and publish your book but how does it work? You see countless indie authors (self-published writers) uploading new books every month, and you're wondering how they're doing it. Better yet, you've got that longing to also be able to call yourself an author.

You want your story to be known. You want to share your very own book with the world!

Well, the good news is, you can certainly do it! And while it took me a year to figure out the entire self-publishing process on my own, I highly recommend you get someone's help to at least get you through the process much more quickly so you can only focus on the writing process and have fun during the editing, publishing and marketing!

Because after all, enjoying being an author is the key! But being an author is not just about writing. True. It is a lot more than that, and so I hope that this book will serve you as a guide to help you get started on this journey to become a full-fledged indie author!

I'll walk you through the steps I used and still use when I write and publish my books from the beginning until the end.

If anything it should get you excited to get started! It's not all that difficult. Anyone can publish a book! But as self-published authors, we have an even bigger responsibility to ensure our manuscript is of the best quality possible, and we do it all. But that's also part of the fun!

We make all the decisions! We call all the shots! The amount of freedom we have as a self-published or indie author is phenomenal and it is, to me, what makes self-publishing so great!

So make yourself comfortable, maybe grab a pen and paper in the event you'd wish to make some notes. You're welcome to use this book as a step by step guide and so read it as you write your manuscript, or you can read it all at once, and then apply what it says when you work on your book.

You're always welcome to contact me at any time at mahinaperrotcoach@gmail.com if you have any questions.

Remember, everyone has their own way of doing things. Here I am telling you about my way of writing, editing and publishing a book, which works for me and all of my clients, but you're always welcome to look for more or different information online, watch Youtube videos and read more books that can help you!

"The book in you"

So, you've always wanted to write a book but you haven't got any clue as to where to start. Or better still, you've got an idea - a brilliant idea, of course! - but you don't know how to write, or you may be thinking that you don't have what it takes to write it.

Perhaps you've managed to finish your first draft ... Or maybe you've only written a few pages but for some unfathomable reason, you feel full of doubts and can't bring yourself to open your word document once again ... There always seem to be more important things to do than to write. Yet you feel that pull towards your manuscript. You can imagine your characters so vividly in your mind that they could be living next door, for all you know. You're thinking about it so much that you wake up at night with some ideas that you write down fervently in a notepad that's always in your bag or pocket.

Yet, when you have some free time and could open that Word document, you can't seem to bring yourself to do it. And when you do, you stare at the screen, and despite your best efforts, the words don't seem to come.

You have come across the infamous writer's block. You then begin to procrastinate. You give it some time so you forget about your book for a couple of days. A few days turn into a few weeks, which turn into a few months which, in the end, turn into a few years until you forget about your book or simply think of it as a dream you've once had but that never came true.

Since you're reading this now, let me tell you that I'm not going to let you let that dream remain just that - a dream.

Together, we will "manifest" - that is bring into this 3D reality or "real world" as everyone defines it - YOUR book! Follow the steps outlined in this book or better yet, get in touch with me, and I guarantee that you'll hold your book in your hand in no time!

If you're determined to keep writing but are not quite sure what your next step should be, if you are confused about the online publishing process, which is still rather new to most people today, or if you believe that the only way you can publish a book is if you spend thousands of dollars on an editor (you don't), this book can help you!

Asking yourself a lot of questions as you write your book is normal! It's part of being human, and, more specifically, part of being a "creative" human being.

Since you're creating something new, a new book, you're moving in a new direction. You're about to bring into existence something which doesn't exist yet! You are a creator, literally. And because you're walking straight into the unknown - since you don't know what your creation will end up looking like - it is natural to feel scared.

But again, you're not alone. I'm here to help. This book is here to help you. I truly hope that you will consider it your loyal companion during the writing and publishing process of your very own book.

You see, we are all creative beings, but some of us are better than others at gathering up the courage needed to start something new, whether it is launching a new business, travelling to unknown places, starting a family, or doing something you've never done before, like writing a book.

But all of us are born with the innate ability to make our dreams come true.

It might take you longer than others, but life is not a race. You're always at the right place at the right time. What's meant to be will always be. So take your time and do what feels right to you.

Simply know that if you feel that intense pull inside of you, that strong desire to write, to express yourself, and to share your very own creation with others, it doesn't matter how long it takes, you will succeed in writing and publishing your own book!

This book was written as a short but concise roadmap to help you navigate the writing and publishing processes as easy as possible so that you can reach your ultimate destination - that of becoming a published author - as easily and enjoyably as possible!

By purchasing it, you have made the conscious decision to embark on this extraordinary, life-changing, journey. Because trust me, it will change your life!

You have decided to set out on this mission which will be to write, finish, edit, design and publish and market your first book in just 90 days!

So, let's make that happen, shall we?

Why you should definitely write it!

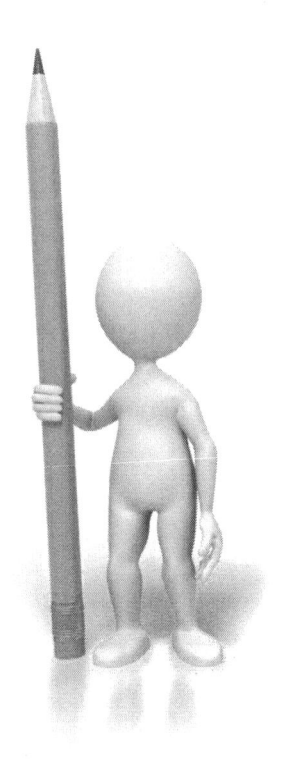

Not everybody feels like writing a book, but, again, I strongly believe that everyone has a story and that it deserves to be shared with the world.

Books truly shape our world and thus, they change our lives. They certainly have shaped and changed mine! Have you heard of the saying: "We are the books we read"?. Does it resonate with you?

Here are some fun questions you can ask yourself too.

What's your favourite book? Has reading it changed your life in any way?

When I was given a book called Jaguar by Alan Rabinowitz, I just knew that I too would someday see jaguars in the wild. And I did.

That book sparked a fire in my heart. It ignited a dream and which I then made true! And not only did I get to see jaguars in their natural habitats in the Pantanal (Brazil), but the author also inspired me to write my book about jaguars, a young adult fiction book called IZEL, the Black Panther.

I even created a young boy character in the book called Azlan, based on this man, as a way to honour him for all the work he does to help these animals!

And I certainly hope that my book will, someday, change someone's life too!

In fact, the mother of a young boy called William who bought the book and read it to him tells me he loves it and keeps talking about it! So who knows if and how my book will shape his world as he grows up?

It might inspire him to care for animals, or to go on adventures as he gets older!

You may also believe that to write a book, you have to be a writer. You have to excel at grammar or have a very wide vocabulary. Not necessarily!

Of course, it helps if the words flow to you easily but thanks to modern-day technology there are a lot of things, such as softwares, apps, etc, that will help you write your book, and thus share your story, or your passions and expertise or skills with the world.

And if your story can inspire even just one person, change the life of one child or help one man or woman make a decision that will allow them to be happier, healthier, more fulfilled, wealthier, more generous, kinder, more compassionate, more loving towards themselves and others, or simply accept themselves for who they are, then it is most definitely worth sharing it!

You would actually do others a disservice if you didn't write that book! So don't let anything or anyone hold you back! You've got what it takes and you've also got all the help you need!

Whatever you feel like writing, whether it is fiction or non-fiction, your book will have a purpose and so, one way or another, it will reach the right people.

You see, writing a book is not just about creating a passive income! Sure, it does mean that you will be able to sell a (fantastic) product, and thus may make some great extra cash. But your book, especially if it is about your personal journey, a transformation you've gone through, or if it dives deep into your passions or defines your business, and reveals your skills and expertise, will allow you to inspire others.

As a business owner or entrepreneur, for instance, publishing a book will allow you to be seen as an expert in your niche or as a leader in your market. It'll add credibility to your business. You may also be called to speak about your book publicly or you may decide to give it to your clients either as a bonus or as part of a package or programme. Your book will help your audience, your clients, your readers understand what you do and why you do it on a much more profound level.

In a sense, a book is a portal or a gateway to that part of yourself and of your soul that you wish to express and share with specific people (your niche) or even with the entire world.

What's more, in our hugely competitive world, where so many of us are doing the same thing, a book allows you to stand out. And it gives your prospective clients another way to find you, in this wide online world.

This is actually how I personally found my own mentor. I came across her trilogy, read it, and felt so inspired by what she had written that I just knew I had to contact her.

That was almost seven years ago and as of today she's still my mentor and has even become a precious friend.

Traditional vs Vanity publishing

While in this book I am going to teach you how to publish your own book, it is still important that we understand the fundamental differences between Traditional publishing, Vanity or Hybrid publishing, and self-publishing (in the next chapter).

Traditional publishing, is still hugely popular, of course, because if your book is chosen by a popular publishing house such as Random House, for instance, it has more chances of becoming a best-seller and of being more widely distributed than other books. The book is also associated with the reputation of the publishing house which can help it quickly gain in popularity.

As a "published author", you will get a "reputation" and should your book excel and become the next Harry Potter, you'll be famous! However, these are very rare instances. We don't know most of the Traditional publishers' names of the books we love to read. For instance, can you tell me where your copy of The Hobbit was published? And because you're published doesn't always mean you'll be featured on TV or that your book will gain instant popularity.

Also, very few publishing houses accept manuscripts directly nowadays. Some do, but you usually have to send it to them by post and they may take up to 6 months to a year to reply to you (usually to say that they're not interested). In the event they are interested in your manuscript, the process of editing, redesigning the book (you don't get much of a say there by the way) etc can take up to two years!

Also, most of the traditional publishers (the real ones) online now require that you go through an agent first.

Please be very careful there and understand that a real agent will never ask you for money. He or she will simply ask for a commission should your book be chosen by one of the publishing houses they present it to. There are several agents' websites online. Most are genuine, yet I strongly recommend that you never send them your entire manuscript.

In fact, never send your full book manuscript over the internet to anyone. Always send them a sample (say 3 or 4 chapters) and if they are interested, they'll contact you and you can talk with them about the best way to send them the entire manuscript.

But beware of scams. In today's online world, I'm afraid to say they are all too common! They are all over the internet and actively prey on enthusiastic aspiring authors.

One of the great things about traditional publishing is that if they accept your book, they will do everything including the editing and proofreading of your book, they may even come up with a cover and/or chapters design and they will be in charge of the marketing and distribution of your book to various book stores (and online too now).

You then get paid by earning "royalties", which as the Oxford dictionary defines as "a certain sum paid to a patentee for the use of a patent or to an author or composer for each copy of a book sold or for each public performance of a work".

The only issue is that it may take a while before you start to earn any money at all. Usually, while they covered all of the initial costs, traditional publishers will need to pay themselves back first before they can offer you your first cheque. So it might take a little while before you get anything at all.

A friend of mine, a retired magazine editor, also a wildlife expert, who wrote a beautifully illustrated and highly detailed textbook about animals, was hugely disappointed when, first of all, the publishers did a terrible job printing the cover with a paper and ink that, in his opinion, really didn't do justice to the picture he has chosen, and then when he got a 600$ cheque six months later.

He said the had been approached by a Vanity publisher and almost wished he had worked with them instead.

Also, a very important thing to consider is that if you choose to go for a traditional publisher, you should be okay with foregoing any publishing rights for the duration of your contract. That is, you will not be able to publish your book anywhere else (even on your website).

You may not even be allowed to "market" or advertise your book and, like a friend of mine whose book got published, you may even be asked, as part of your contract, to not comment on or review any books by any other authors! She even had to delete every single review of books she had written before, on Amazon and elsewhere!

As crazy as it sounds, it is something that some traditional publishers require. Whatever happens though, I strongly recommend that you ensure you always keep your copyrights and that under no circumstances, unless you're happy with it, of course, do you relinquish them to anyone.

If you wish to have your book available in the public domain then you are welcome to do that, but if you give all of your copyrights to a publishing company it means they will own the totality of your book. As such if, for instance, someone decides to turn your book into a movie, you would then not be able to have any say as to how it is adapted and, of course, you wouldn't be able to earn any commission either (or at least won't be allowed to negotiate anything).

If you choose to work with what is known as Vanity Publishers, be very careful.

A Vanity press or Vanity publisher, sometimes also called a Hybrid or Subsidy publisher, is legal but they are publishing "houses" or companies which authors have to pay to have their books published.

If you check online reviews of some Vanity publishers, you'll find that a lot of them are accused of being scams and have a very bad reputation.

This is mostly due to the fact, first of all, they'll charge a very large amount of money for their "services". The problem here is that there is no way to verify if they are promoting your book and where. You don't know how visible you are "out there".

What's more, most of them offer to put up your book on an online platform like Amazon or Barnes and Nobles, which is something you can do on your own, and they will be reluctant as soon as you start mentioning the fact you'd like your book to be available in book stores as most of them prefer to operate online.

It's easier and less traceable, and of course, way cheaper and less work for them. However, if you find one that has an actual, physical office which you can visit, in a town or city and they guarantee that your book is going to be available in book stores all over the place, and you can afford their services, then it could be something you'd like to consider and they may do a very good job.

As part of their package, they will usually include editing and proofreading services, you may be able to have more of a say as to what the cover of your book may look like but they might also offer you the possibility of having a professional designer doing the cover, and many also offer Audiobook conversions and book trailers. Some also offer to create a professional author's website for you.

The website selfpublishing.com offers some valuable insights and has a list of the top publishers to avoid, which you may want to have a look at if you are ever contacted by a "publisher" (which you probably will once you self-publish your book).

When they are not asking for money upfront, Vanity or Hybrid publishers may instead ask you for 500 printed copies of your book for them to distribute (but you don't know what price they're selling it for, and where they're selling them from).

So again, be very careful. They are very good at coming directly to you! One day you'll pick up the phone and this person will tell you they have read your book and loved it and they will go on and on about how they'd like to publish your boo. They'll get you very excited about this opportunity, and then send you a contract to sign after one or two emails or calls.

Please, make sure you read their contract properly before signing anything! Also, while most of them are not illegal, others have been using the same "system" or pretending to be Vanity publishers to scam gullible new authors who truly believe someone is keen to publish their book!

Before doing anything, check them out online, look at their reviews. When I looked up one of such companies that contacted me, I saw that someone had complained about his dying grandmother having been told to pay one such company 7000$ to publish her collection of poems. She had sent the money but neither she nor her grandson had ever heard from that company again!

That comment was written as a review alongside other terrible reviews but the company didn't respond or seem to care (and if they're scammers, they just wouldn't respond since all they need to do is to change their companies' name and do it again!). So just be wary of anything that seems "too good to be true"!

Of course, you always have a choice! There are pros and cons to everything in life so the ultimate decision is up to you and to chat you want to do.

Why self-publishing Is the best

Personally, I would always recommend self-publishing. While being a self-published author may have been considered "trashy" in the past, it is not the case - at all - anymore.

Plenty of self-published authors have made it to the top and can make a real living from it. According to an Amazon's 2019 review of its Kindle sales, thousands of self-published authors are taking home royalties of over $50,000 and more than a thousand hit six-figure salaries from their book sales in 2020!

Many self-published authors have been extremely successful. Lawyer-turned-writer L.J Ross, the author of Holy Island, for example, has become hugely popular and has now published no less than 19 novels and has now sold a total of around 4.5 million copies!

Rachel Abbott's first book, Only The Innocent, was at the top of the Kindle store just three months after she published it in 2011. Number-one New York Times best-selling author Leigh Bardugo, the author of the hugely popular fantasy saga The Shadow and bone, has had her book adapted by Netflix.

And there are many, many more such examples. I'm not saying that you can leave your current job or that you'll become famous and wealthy as soon as you'll self-published, but this shows that it is possible to make a living from being a self-published author.

It is what allows pretty much anyone with wonderful ideas to get those out for the world to read about!

On the other hand, you don't necessarily need to want to become a full-time author to write and publish your book! And this is where self-publishing becomes really interesting.

Today, anyone and everyone can upload their book on Amazon. And this means three things:

Firstly, authors take responsibility for what they publish.

As an author, you have to ensure that you are releasing a high-quality product. Indeed, readers can leave reviews so you want to make sure your book is as perfect as it can be; that you share high-value content, that you have edited your book properly and that you come up with a visually appealing design.

Secondly, self-publishing also means that you have to do everything! You do all the work but it's part of the fun!

As a self-published author, you are free to write about anything you want! The amount of freedom you get as a self-published author is truly refreshing! You get to decide the length of your book, its style and genre, as well as its design, its cover, its audience, its price - everything!

You get to set your price and get the royalties on KDP accordingly, or you can choose to sell your books in your local book store. You choose how you market and sell your book and so the chances of getting a passive income, when done right, are actually higher than with the other types of publishing.

As a business owner, entrepreneur, this is a wonderful opportunity to share your expertise, make your readers want to get to know you more. If you've always wanted to write children's books, you can do that! If you're been on a transformational journey and want to share it, you can do that too!

Also, you don't have to write anything too lengthy or too complex. You don't even have to stick to a genre at all if you don't want to! Remember here though, that your readers will expect certain things, so don't market your book as a thriller if it is a romantic comedy, obliviously, but let's say you want to write a story for kids, nothing stops you now from including games in your book, or from using various fonts or colours!

When turning your book into a Kindle file, you can even add links to your website, to your Youtube channel or any other file you'd like your readers to get access to as well!

And even though there are no guarantee self-publishers are actual writers, I've read a lot of excellent self-published books. And don't forget, the people whose books are published by traditional houses are not necessarily writers either!

Yet, just like with any other "profession", it is also easy for people who want to "make a quick buck" to publish terrible books or mislead their readers.

I remember being asked to review a book that was supposedly about how to deal with the Covid Crisis but the book contained - I'm not joking - about 5% written words and all the rest consisted of simple, empty lines. I quickly understood that it was designed to be used as a journal, so it had a few, short questions at the beginning of each chapter, and tons of lines in between!

Now, I wouldn't have particularly minded that, had I known that this book was to be used in such a way. But the description was very misleading as I thought the book was going to be a psychological discussion almost of what it feels like to be in lock-down and that it would give me actual tips on how to overcome the potential obstacles that came with being in such a situation.

Luckily such books are not that common, and terrible books (unfortunately or fortunately) usually get bad reviews very quickly. Also, thanks to the Kindle App (which you can download for free - you don't need to buy a Kindle) you can preview a few pages of the book before purchase.

I hadn't done that when asked to review that book as I was able to download it for free during one of the author's Kindle promotions, but in any other cases, if you're not sure whether you'll like the book or not, you can do that. Just download a sample and read it through first.

Of course, for authors, this means that you need to hook the reader in at the very beginning of your book!

And the thing is, you don't need to be the greatest of writers to publish a great book! Everyone is capable of writing and publishing a high-quality book, as long as they put in the necessary effort and seek the necessary help when required.

If you only have great ideas but need someone to write your book for you, you can always hire a ghost writer.

If you write your book in Spanish and need it to be published in English, you can hire a translator. Hiring an editor or at the very least a proofreader can also make a huge difference. Or you can simply follow the steps I outline in this book and still manage to do a fantastic job self-editing your book.

As with anything else in life, practice makes better but finding joy in the journey is also what will help you write your best book! Write something you're passionate about and your book's energy or vibration or intention will be instantly apparent.

Also, once you've published your book, you'll notice that the more good reviews you get, the more sales you make, the more fulfilled you'll feel too, knowing that your book has reached that amount of people.

That's another great thing about self-publishing, you get to see exactly how many people are buying your book!

So, now that you know all about the various types of publishing and understand why I choose to self-publish, let's embark on this new exciting adventure together as I guide you through the 12 steps that I have personally designed to write and publish your first book in just 90 days!

About me

You may be wondering, how can I be sure that these steps will help you? Because I use these very steps to write and publish my books!

It took me a little while to come up with these steps. I've made probably all of the mistakes self-published authors who try to do everything on their make, and I've learned a lot along the way. And my goal now is to help you so that you don't do the same mistakes and can create and release your book as effortlessly and efficiently as possible!

I am lucky in the sense that I do have experience as a writer, having graduated in 2009 with a Bachelor in Communication Studies and a Major in Journalism. I've worked for several magazines, newspapers and online websites over the last 15 years so I am familiar with the writing, editing and publishing processes.

I had always wanted to become an author but it wasn't until Covid 19 hit and I lost my job in the Tourism Industry that I finally had the time to make that dream come true!

Since I am a very determined person, when I decided to launch myself as an author, I dived into it 1000 %. A dear friend of mine even nicknamed me the "Tahitian Tornado" (I grew up in Tahiti) as I kept on writing one book after another!

In total, I published a total of nine books in just seven months. The first books I wrote were children's books which I also illustrated and translated (in French, in English and then I did Bilingual versions as well).

I then wrote a little biography, Wild Adventures, which is a compilation of funny and sometimes even scary anecdotes of my encounters with wild animals during my travels as a wildlife journalist.

Once I finished this one, I picked up a manuscript I had started ten years ago and which I desperately wanted to finish but had never been able to. And I decided that this time I would finish it.

As I was trying to finish that one, another book idea came to me and this one was so easy for me to write that I knew then I had found my "writer's voice". I finished and published Manifesting: A simple yet powerful step-by-step guide to creating the successful and abundant life your desire within just three weeks!

Once this one was done I went back to the manuscript that was the most difficult for me to finish. I had written several books already but finishing this young adult fiction which I had started to write ten years previously was definitely one of the most challenging things I have ever done in my entire life!

The book, called IZEL the Black Panther, tells the story of the first black jaguar born in the Amazon rainforest. Because I had been thinking about that book for so many years, by the time I finished the manuscript, the characters in it were pretty much "alive" to me!

And there are simply no words that could describe the euphoric feeling I experienced when I finally completed it. It was beyond anything I had every felt before!

Writing all of these books has been extremely challenging yet hugely fulfilling! The whole journey has been exhilarating.

And I firmly believe that this is what life should be about - enjoying the journey and making it count, all while expressing ourselves as much as we can!

Now, while I did the hard work and learned the hard way, I need to mention a very important fact. It wasn't just my efforts that allowed me to achieve such a feat. You see, I had tried to write and publish books before, but it never worked.

Yes, I had more time to write and I was determined to making it happen. So I would, one way or another. But that's when the Universe or God seems to step in. For some reason, a fellow author and wildlife photographer who was genuinely interested in my work and would spend hour reading my manuscripts one after the other as I finished them.

He quickly became a friend, and a mentor and coach in a way. He always supported me, encouraged me, believed in me, and pushed me past all of my self-imposed limiting beliefs.

We also published a book together called Foxy's wild adventures, which tells the story of a little wild fox as he learns about the big wide world, and we used his photographs of real foxes to illustrate it. He even designed to cover of my book IZEL the Black Panther!

His help was truly invaluable and without him, I wouldn't have achieved all that. He made all the difference!

Trust me, I wanted to give up so many times. But I refused. I didn't. I decided to go on, and keep pushing, mostly because I knew he was watching. Not that he would judge me, I'm sure he would have been proud and happy for me whatever I did (or didn't do) as long as I'm happy, but I felt I had to make him proud, and he made me want to make myself proud!

Yes, it was hard, but I becoming an author was yet another dream I wanted to make true. And so I did - as you will too!

As a result, not only did I publish all of those amazing books which I love so much, but it even led me on a completely new personal journey as i realised what I truly wanted to be and do.

Without realising it, my friend had inspired me not just to become the author I've always wanted to be, but to also help other people who wish to write and publish their book make that happen.

The 12-step process

Today, I am thrilled to be working with a wide range of fantastic clients. These are mostly soulful entrepreneurs and passionate business owners who want to share their journey, their passions, their thoughts and their skills with the world!

I am also dedicated to helping them all achieve their goal of writing and publishing their first book within just 90 days, and so far it has been a huge success.

When I work with people, I help them stay on track, stay motivated and hold them accountable so they complete a step every week.

Because I have written quite a few books in a short amount of time, I was actually able to see a pattern clearly emerge as to how I could most efficiently write and publish my books and this pattern or process is what I am about to share with you.

By the way, if you do decide that you want to work one on one with me, you are always welcome to contact me at mahinaperrotcoach@gmail.com, or check out my 12-week Quantum Writer Programme: https://www.mahinaperrot.com/quantum-writer/

By using the code 90DAYS you will get an instant 50% off the entire programme!

When you work with me you not only get to understand all 12 steps that I go through in this book on a whole other and much deeper level, but we also do private 1:1 consultations each week, and I am here to help you every step of the way as you write and publish your book.

As a bonus, I also proofread your manuscript and can even help you design the cover. What's more, as a Quantum manifestation Coach, I work a lot with frequencies and believe in the power of sound so as part of the Quantum Writer, you also get 12 unique and powerful frequencies that you can use to reprogramme your brain, remove conscious and unconscious blockages and boost your creativity and productivity.

You also have full access to me for 12 weeks, and two extra follow-up sessions during which I help you set up a marketing strategy to promote your book.

Of course, you can do it on your own too, and if you are committed to your goal and follow those steps diligently, you will succeed!

However, if your goal is to write a fiction book, you should be thinking of writing and publishing your book in six months, not three.

Everyone's writing skills and speed are different, obliviously, but while short children's books, biographies, transformational journeys, guidebooks, recipe books etc can usually be completed within those 12 weeks using this process, I'd recommend that anyone writing fiction books, thrillers, fantasy or science-fiction doubles that time frame. This means that rather than completing one step in one week, I'd recommend you take two weeks per step.

That said, if you go through those 12 steps thoroughly, you will still be able to write and publish your book within six months, which is still pretty amazing!

Now, let's talk about the 12 steps process!

You will find that there are two parts to each of these steps. The first dimension has to do with your mindset. Because writing a book is not something you do mechanically. It is instinctive and graceful. The words should flow from you, and the process should both feel natural and contain the right amount of pressure to challenge you and keep you going.

And of course, I also focus on the technical sides of the job and teach my clients all there is to know about the actual writing, editing, designing, publishing and marketing processes.

Step 1: Choose

So what's the first and probably most important thing you must do when you want to write a book? It is to choose! Yes, really, I mean it, choose!

Choose what? Well, choose to write that book of yours! Before you do anything else, you have to make the conscious decision to choose to write a book! You have to commit to that decision as if your life depends on it!

As human beings, we have the ability to be conscious of our own choices. You get to choose! No one is telling you to write that book!

It's your choice, right? It's something you desire, that you want? Still, you have to choose.

It takes effort to choose because it means you then have a responsibility to see things through until the end, and it takes even more effort to keep choosing every step of the way.

But when you don't give up, and remember that you always have a choice and that writing this book is your idea, your choice, and something that only you can do, you are taking your power back as the conscious creator of your reality. You want to create something and you, and only you, have the ability and potential to bring this unique book into existence!

Just making a choice and deciding that you'll write your book in just 90 days is exciting and fulfilling in itself!

So make a conscious choice. What is it that you really want? Write it down! Say it out loud! Your commitment if you're reading this right now should be to write and publish your first book, or second book, or third book, wherever you're at, in just 90 days!

Commit to making it happen! Commit to your success! And guess what, it will become reality! So your number one task is to write all these down:

" I choose to write and publish my book in 90 days!"

"I choose to commit to my success!"

" I choose to make my dreams come true!"

"I choose to make it happen"

"I choose to give it my all"

"I choose to succeed no matter what"

You can write them all on one sheet of paper, or several, you can add them to your phone but as a wallpaper, not in notes where you'll just forget about them, or as a desktop on your laptop. Do whatever works for you.

The goal is to put them somewhere you can see them every day.

If you like to have that list by your bedside table, pick it up every morning and every night and repeat those affirmations in your mind or out loud.

This is certainly the most important step in this whole process because your choices define your future.

What you choose now shapes your outside world and your circumstances and has consequences. Choose to succeed and you will be successful. Choose to commit to doing everything in your power to actually write and publish your first book in 90 days and you will make it happen!

Now, the next important thing you've got to decide, that falls under this chapter, is obviously the topic of your book.

You may have plenty of ideas, and you're welcome to write them all down, but you're going to have to choose one story, one set of skills, one journey you've been through, one thing that you will be writing about first.

Remember, once you've written your first book, it will become even easier for you to write the next one, and the next. So be still for a moment, take some deep breaths, and consider: What it is you really want to write about?

What is one thing you could talk about all day long?
What is so important to you that you want to share it with others?

What do you specialise in/what are your top skills, that you know people would benefit from reading about?

What transformation have you gone through in your life?

What invaluable lessons have you learned and found valuable in life?

What makes you stand out? What do people say about you that resonates with you (or not)?

What do you care about?

What do you dream of?

What do you want people to feel when they read your book?

What books do you personally enjoy? Why?

The truth is, if you're here now if you're reading this book, it is most likely because you're feeling called to write. You want to share something, and you probably already know what it is.

Even if what you want to do is write fiction, you are still expressing a part of yourself. And that is the ultimate purpose of writing! By being yourself, and truly using your favourite medium - in that case, a book - to share a part of your soul, you will have accomplished something amazing, beautiful, and very important.

I sincerely believe it is part of the reason why you were born, and why you are so unique. Your message, your story, your book will be as unique as you are!

Just like an artist's painting, your book will fall into the hands of the readers who will love and be inspired by your work.

Now that you are committed to making this dream to write and publish your own book in 90 days, and that you have decided WHAT you want to write about, you need to consider your big WHY.

Finding out the WHY behind what you are writing is what will make the whole process truly enjoyable!

If writing a book is something others expect you to do, or if you are doing it solely because you want to generate a passive income, get more clients, or create a quick freebie to give away, then you are lacking something fundamental, and it won't have the depth of a book that is written with a pure, loving intention.

As a result, it most likely won't reach the audience you want.

Let's remember for a moment that we are all energetic beings. We are all energy. Like I mentioned earlier, as a Quantum Manifestation Coach, as well as a Writing Coach, when I work with clients one on one, we touch on every dimension of book writing, especially on that energetic dimension.

We use very specific frequencies to imbue every step of this process with the energies that you need to allow you to quantum leap and create a high-vibration book which then acts like a magnet to attract the perfect readers.

It obviously is a very personal process, and so you are always welcome to book a call with me if you want to expand on this topic and also work with energies during the writing and publishing processes.

However, I will say that if you write with, for example, a desperate intention or if your big WHY is not aligned with who you truly are and/or with the pure intention of serving others or helping other people, no matter what it may bring you back in return, the energy you are sending out will be murky, and flawed.

It will contain some desperate "detritus" as I personally call it.

If we consider that we are all energetic magnets and that we infuse everything we do with energy depending on what we feel, the more you are able to clear your energy and define the powerful reason as to why you are writing this book, the more easily the words will come to you, and of course the more your readers will enjoy it and the more successful you will be. Not just at writing books but at everything that you do.

So take some time to clear your energy. Remove all layers of other people's expectations, of false or limiting beliefs and find within you the real reason why you feel called to write this particular book.

Here are some questions that can help you define that big WHY:

What is it that you long to express?

Why does this book matter so much to you?

Why, in your opinion, would people benefit from reading it?

Why would they pick up your book on the shelf and not someone else's?

Why did you decide or feel called to write in the first place?

Why is it so important to you?

Even if no one ever read your book, would you still feel the call to write it? Why?

Then, as you come up with all of these answers, as yourself HOW you feel about writing this book.

How do you feel when you write about this particular topic or share your unique story?

How would you feel if you could hold your book in your own hands now?

How does it feel to see other people holding your book or reading it?

How does it feel to see the 5-star reviews about your book?

How do you feel talking to others about your book?

So step one, or week one, is all about asking yourself those very important questions. You will begin to get a real sense of what you want to write about and perhaps even of what your book will look and feel like once it is published.

Again, if you are writing fiction, you can allow yourself up to two weeks to go through this process.

Make sure you write down the answers to these questions in a notebook that is dedicated to the 12 steps I am taking you through, so you can go back to them whenever you need to.

Also don't forget to do your "I choose..." affirmations twice a day, in the morning and in the afternoon.

And now that you have an idea, and that you have fully defined why you want to bring this book into this 3D reality, you are ready to get started!

Personal Tip: One thing I've learned along the way is that you may have a great idea, and start to write, but as you do so, other things might come up, you might have other ideas or something you hadn't even realised you wanted to write about pops up in your mind and you feel compelled to write about this first.

If you ever feel that you want to change course, even if you are in the middle of the whole writing process, it is absolutely fine! You may have discovered there is something else, something more important and deeper you may actually want to share.

All you need to do is put the manuscript you had started to the side, and begin the new one.

Yes, consistency is key, as we will see in Step 3, which is all about planning, but remember that writing is still a very instinctive process so whenever you can, go with the flow and do what feels right to you.

So, this first step was all about starting to build momentum. Just like a fire starts with just a few sparks, you will now start to add more and more coal to your inner fire, and ultimately, it will roar to life!

Step 2: Research

Once you've figured out what you want your book to be about, and the big why behind it, you will, of course, need to do a bit of research.

Why now? Because if you wait, you will most likely waste a lot of time later on. Trust me, I've been there. I will be sharing with you what I know about the writing and publishing process here but I also recommend that you get extra curious and take about a week (two for fiction writers) to gather as much information as you need so you can begin writing on the right foot.

1. Get a notebook

From now on, I suggest that you always walk around with a little notebook that is fully dedicated to your book.

You can also use your Notes app on your phone, just make sure that as soon as you have an idea, you write it down.

This is very useful even though you will find that you may never go back to your notes because the information you'll have written there will either not be useful or will have been stored in your subconscious brain; it is also very likely that some of these ideas will become chapter titles, or may even inspire you to write more books later on.

2. Figure out the WHO?

Indeed, now that you know what you'll write and why you want to write it, you need to take some time to consider exactly who your audience will be. Who is going to read your book?

Asking yourself the following questions might help:

Who exactly are you writing the book for?

How old is your ideal reader?

What do they do?

What do they enjoy most?

What do they really want to know about? your story?
Scientific facts? Anecdotal evidence? Practical advice? A bit of everything?

What would make your book invaluable to them?

Why would the reader want to read a book written by you?

Interestingly, you can also do this process the other way around. You can begin to write and once you've found your voice, once the words are flowing and you're writing in a style that suits you, you can then look at other similar books and see who they were written for, or even ask friends and family members who they think this book would appeal to most.

Of course, you should do what feels best for you, but having an idea of who is going to read your book will help you in the long run, when you want to, for example, prepare targeted ads or do book readings.

If you are a business owner or entrepreneur and you have decided to write your book for your clients, it wouldn't hurt to begin to look for two or three "beta readers" now.

These are the people - preferably your "ideal readers" - who would be willing to read your manuscript and give you feedback before it is published.

They can be people you know well or total strangers. It doesn't matter as long as they guarantee you they'll give you sincere feedback!

3. What's your book's genre?

The next step is to start to read more about the genre you have decided to write about.

This is a tricky one though. On the one hand, I believe that, since you are self-publishing, you should go with the flow and really write in a style and way that is unique to you and suits you. So don't necessarily compare your writing style to others, or don't feel you have to write like other people.

For example, self-help books are a genre, but their styles vary widely, so pick up a few that you like and "be like a sponge". Soak in the information, the colours, the look and feel of the books you really enjoy, and then "keep in mind" only what feels best to you.

Business books tend to be similar. There are so many out there and they are all very different, and very unique. So again, don't limit yourself.

Self-publishing is really amazing in that it allows you total freedom when it comes to the way your book will look.

It only becomes a bit more complicated when you decide to write a very specific genre, such as fantasy, fiction, science-fiction, mystery, thriller, romance, children's books, young adult fiction, etc.

If you do want to write such a book, then of course, while you should let your imagination run wild and create whatever story you feel inspired to create, you should most definitely research how to write plots, dialogues, etc properly.

You can research your genre online or ask your local librarian, university professors, or even a fellow author for advice on the genre you enjoy most. Find out as much as you can about how to best create and develop your characters, your plot, what's the overall "map" of each book or genre, what makes a successful book and more.

The second most important thing to do at this stage as well is to read as many books written in that particular genre as possible. This feeds what I call your "inner writer", the instinctive writer within you so that when you actually get started, everything flows a lot more easily.

If you are writing about your personal experience, your biography, something that happened to you, a transformational journey of sorts, or if you're writing a guidebook, then go with what feels good to you!

Another thing you can do right now is to start to get a feel at what your end product will be like. So, for example, what will your book look like once it is printed? Look at books that inspire you, and take some notes.

What book covers do you like most?

What colour palettes do your favourite authors use?

How light or dense is the paper/cover of these types of books?

Are the books thick, light? Do they use small or big fonts? Fancy or traditional fonts?

What do you like most about these books?

How many chapters do such books contain?

How many pages does each chapter have?

How many pages does the overall book contain?

What made you pick this one over another?

What format do these books use?

4. Decide on the format - now!

Then, put your notes together and decide what format your book will be.

It's important to consider this now so that you don't write your whole book in a particular format and end up having written say 220 pages, but when you upload it or put it in an A5 printed book format, it ends up being a 1400-page book, which is way too big and which means you'll have a lot of editing to do.

Here are a few guidelines which you can use to start with.

If you use KDP (Kindle Direct Publishing), which I personally use and will be talking to you about in this book, you need to know two things:

- You will need a pdf file of your book to upload when printing your paperback (so it'll need to be sized and formatted properly first).

- You will need a Kpf (or Epub) file of your book if you want to also have a Kindle version of your book (this can be done easily using the Kindle Create app but by uploading a Doc or Docx file).

Both paperback and Kindler versions are actually very different, and you'll find that you pretty much end up creating two different books.

I've had to go through this process for all of my nine books so, believe me, if you don't think about those things now, you may end up feeling so overwhelmed at the end. So much so that it may, like it has for so many aspiring writers, discourage you from publishing your book even though you are so close!

But don't panic, as I am here to help you.

PAPERBACK Version

If you want to publish a paperback, which most people do, first ask yourself:

What size do you want your book to be?

How many pages (approximately) will your book have?

Will it contain pictures? Quotes? Anything unusual?

How big do you want the font to be?

Once you have a pretty good idea as to what you want, you will need to make sure that the word document you are using is of the right size.

Personal Tip: By the way, ALWAYS use Word (Pack Office) or WPS (Mac). Do NOT use Notes or Google Docs to write your book, as it will make everything harder for you in the long run if you do.

Now, once you have your book open in a Word or WPS document, look for "Layout" or "Page Layout" (see picture) and choose "Size". Then choose the size of the format you wish your book to be.

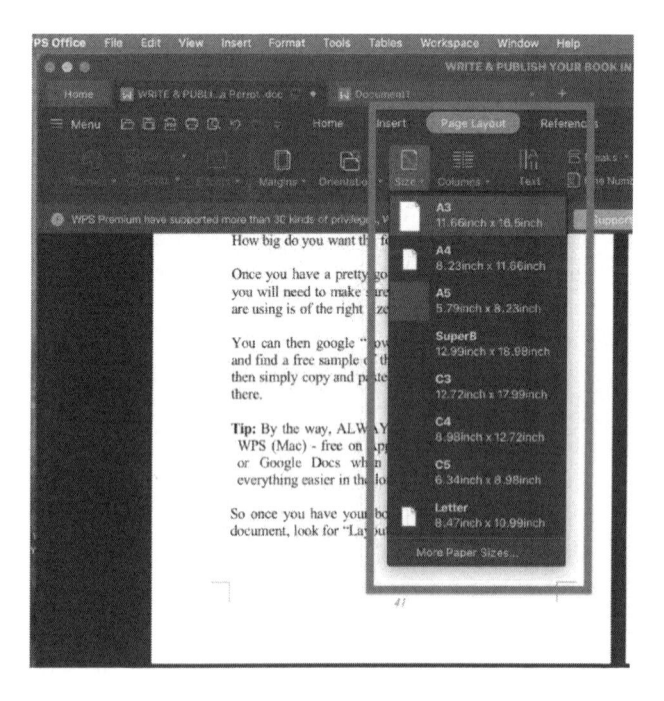

But how do you choose which format is best? Just look at the types of books you like! KDP offers quite a lot of different options as you can see in the images below.

You can choose if you want your book to be printed in black and white or in colour. They also give you options later on as to whether you want it to have a matt or glossy cover.

Here are all of the sizes that KDP, or Amazon, offers so you can compare those with the ones you choose in your Word or WPS document. Make sure they match so that when you upload the pdf file, it is already of the size you will select when uploading your book (more on that later).

Trim Size

Most Popular Standard Trim Sizes:

5 x 8 in	5.25 x 8 in	5.5 x 8.5 in	6 x 9 in
12.7 x 20.32 cm	13.34 x 20.32 cm	13.97 x 21.59 cm	15.24 x 22.86 cm

More Standard Trim Sizes: Compare all standard sizes

5.06 x 7.81 in	6.14 x 9.21 in	6.69 x 9.61 in	7 x 10 in
12.85 x 19.84 cm	15.6 x 23.39 cm	16.99 x 24.4 cm	17.78 x 25.4 cm
7.44 x 9.69 in	7.5 x 9.25 in	8 x 10 in	8.5 x 11 in
18.9 x 24.61 cm	19.05 x 23.5 cm	20.32 x 25.4 cm	21.59 x 27.94 cm

Non Standard Trim Sizes:
These sizes have limited distribution options. How is my book affected?

8.27 x 11.69 in	8.25 x 6 in	8.25 x 8.25 in	8.5 x 8.5 in
21 x 29.7 cm	20.96 x 15.24 cm	20.96 x 20.96 cm	21.59 x 21.59 cm

Self Define Trim Size:
Set up your book with your own trim size.

in ▾ Width: ____ Height: ____ Select

Once you've decided on what size you want your book to be, go ahead and resize your Word or WPS document.

Then go to "Insert" and choose "Insert Page Numbers". You can choose whether you want them centred at the bottom of the page or elsewhere.

Including your page number is always helpful and something we tend to forget to do in the very beginning.

Once that's done, go back to your document and do this:

Pages 1 and 2: Make sure you leave these blank

Page 3: Write your full name (author) and then in the middle of that page your title and underneath your subtitle, if you have one.

Page 4: Leave this page for the disclaimer (you can find an example of disclaimers online or check with your local library) and for your ISBN (Amazon or KDP gives you one for free)

Page 5: You can start to write your book on the 5th page.

Now it's also handy to only begin numbering your pages from the moment your story begins. In that case, simply click on the Header area of your book on the page on which your story starts and add numbers there, but make sure you still leave the previous pages as described previously, to ensure looks good once it's printed.

Last page of your manuscript: Leave some space at the bottom of the last page of your manuscript to add the following:

ISBN

Printed on: Amazon.com

Legal deposit: MONTH / YEAR

You can then close your document for now, and keep it on your desktop or, better still, create a special folder (called MY BOOK or anything you want) and put all of your documents, research etc in there.

Don't forget to set indentation for your book by selecting your whole manuscript and then setting indentation by going to Format > Paragraph and there, under "indentation", and by "Left", type 0.5 under "Special" and then choose "First Line" from the drop-down menu.

Please note that usually, the first paragraph of any chapter after a heading is not indented.

Of course, there are many more things to consider when creating your manuscript, especially if you want to add pictures etc, but this is a good way to start.

Once you've got that done, you can focus on letting your ideas flow and begin to write the first draft of your first book!

KINDLE Version

Now, if you also plan to publish your book on Kindle, this is the time to download Kindle Create:

https://www.amazon.com/Kindle-Create/b?ie=UTF8&node=18292298011

You will also find it easily by searching "Kindle Create App" on Google.

Like I said before, even though you're writing one book, you will be working on two very different manuscripts. It may seem annoying, but having your book on Kindle has enormous benefits.

You can sell it for a lesser price, which many readers appreciate, and still, make a profit as you decide on the price yourself, and having a Kindle version allows you to reach a lot more readers, especially if you add your book to KDP Select (which allows your book to be distributed all over Amazon to people who have a Kindle Unlimited membership, and you get paid per pages read).

So it is totally up to you whether you want to create a Kindle version of your book or not but Kindle books are unique in that you can zoom in or select words, highlight paragraphs, save notes, and link chapters to make it easier for the readers to go straight to a particular page, and so much more. These are all important features to all Kindle book readers.

Now, you could simply convert your pdf file into a Kpf (or Epub) file using a free online software, but personally, I recommend using Kindle Create and taking the time to not just convert your file but add each paragraph carefully to ensure it looks great and works perfectly.

This is something I do in private recorded sessions with my clients to ensure they do this properly and can go back on this when, for example, they write their second book, but with time and dedication you too can succeed in creating a proper Kindle version.

Whatever you do, however, do not upload a simple Pdf or Word doc into KDP for your Kindle book. I made that mistake once and when I purchased my book and downloaded it to "see what it looked like", I was shocked that the writing not only looked tiny, but I couldn't zoom in or do anything with the book.

Each page was like a "picture" that was frozen and it was tiny and simply impossible to read! Also, even though I re-uploaded a Kindle Create Kpf version, later on, the file of the book I had originally purchased was never updated. This means that if someone bought my book when it was published as a pdf file, they would only ever have access to that useless version of the book!

So, don't make the same mistakes!

It may seem time-consuming, but it'll save you time and energy in the long run!

ISBN

As the website ISBN.org states, an ISBN, or International Standard Book Number, is "a 13-digit number that uniquely identifies books and book-like products published internationally."

You will find all of the information you need on ISBNs right here: https://www.isbn.org/faqs_general_questions

But basically an ISBN acts as an identification number. It is rather expensive to purchase (around 125$ last time I checked) and the important thing to remember is that you must have a different ISBN for every format that you use.

So let's say you want to print your book as a paperback (softcover), it will have its unique different ISBN. But if you also have a Hardcover version, that one will have a different ISBN (even though it's the same manuscript, it is not considered the same book since it doesn't look the same, and thus they both have different identification numbers).

Kindle books are not always required to have an ISBN (such as on Amazon for example), but make sure you double-check if you publish your book on other online platforms as some may require even Ebooks to have their ISBN.

What's fantastic about Amazon is that when you use KDP, it gives you an ISBN for free, as long as you use it only for books published on Amazon.

If you want to make your manuscripts available on, say, Barnes and Noble, you will either need to see if they give you one for free there too (and make sure you change the ISBN inside your manuscript and save it again as a pdf with the right ISBN before uploading it there) or, if not, you will need to buy your own.

Buying your own means that, no matter where you sell your book, you can track where it is sold and how many copies are sold. If you use another company's ISBN, you won't be able to access such information.

So whatever you choose is up to you. I do not buy ISBNs and I use those provided by KDP since I publish my books on Amazon. I also use another platform called Bookelis but they too provide authors with a (different) free ISBN for the manuscripts I upload and sell on their website.

Copyrights

Another thing that is important to note is that various countries have different regulations when it comes to owning the copyright of your book.

I strongly suggest that you research carefully how you can own your book's copyright in your own country so that no one can re-use, re-print or plagiarise your manuscript.

In France, for example, I have to register my book on the National Library's website and then send them between 1 and 3 printed copies of my books (depending on how many I sell and where I sell them) which are then stored there and which automatically means that I owe the copyrights of the printed material under my name there.

It also means that I am not allowed to change the content or cover or size or format of my own books wherever I sell them. If I do they need to have another ISBN and I need to re-send them a copy!

Also to be an author, I had to open my own company, by law. Also, when you fill out your bank details to get paid your royalties on KDP, they will ask you for a TAX number so you need to have the number of a registered company. The same applies to Barnes and Nobles, and probably many others.

So make sure you read all of the information on the platform where you decide to publish your book because, for instance, not complying with my country's regulations and not sending my book to the French National Library in France means I could be fined up to 70 000 Euro if they found out (something I'd rather avoid so sending them copies of my book and registering properly is a small price to pay to be legally allowed to sell my books).

Of course, if you are not selling many books, that's usually not a big issue, but the moment your books start to sell well it might become a problem. So the best way to do things is to do is comply with your local laws from the very beginning!

Step 3: Plan

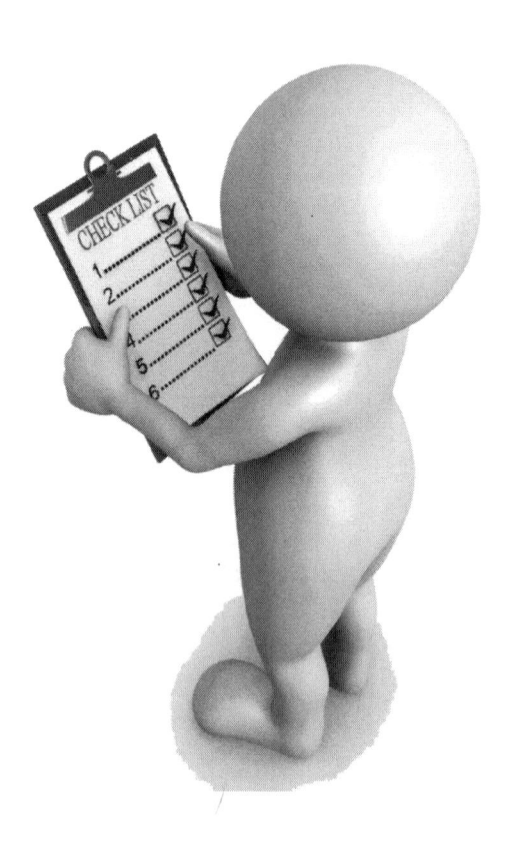

Whether you have already started to write your book or not (and if so, great! But if not, it's absolutely fine!) the next important step is to plan.

So this week (or over the next two weeks if you're writing fiction), you should first begin to assess how many words you think you can write each day or each week.

This will obviously depend on your own personal schedule, and how much time you can allocate to your writing in order to ensure you will write and publish your book in 90 days.

I normally go through this with my clients, but there are several ways you can do this on your own.

Figure out your writing routine.

Write for half an hour every day for five days and/or write purely instinctively over the next week. Then on the 7th day, try and assess:

What time of the day do you feel most inspired to write?

How much time are you able to focus on writing without being distracted?

What works best for you (writing for half an hour every day? An hour every three days? Two hours on a Saturday morning or at night?)

How many words are you (approximately) able to write in half an hour when you are "in the flow", that is when words come to you easily?

Then do some calculations. Let's say you manage to write 2000 words per hour but you found that you prefer to write without being interrupted for two consecutive hours every Saturday evening.

This means you will be able to write, on average 4000 words per week (two hours a week) which means that, if all goes well, you'll have written about 16 000 words in a month or in 4 weeks.

While I am outlining a 12-step process, let's not forget that I take you through the research, planning, writing, editing, designing, publishing and marketing processes of your book, which is a lot.

But the goal is to have about four weeks during which you can focus on your writing only! So calculating how much you'll be able to write in a month is a good start!

Just to give you an example, my book called MANIFESTING: A simple yet powerful step-by-step guide to creating the abundant life you desire is 27887-word long (215-pages) - In reality, it's a bit longer, but only because I added 30 special motivational "cards" at the end.

Now, the number of words you write doesn't really matter. This exercise only aims to give you an idea as to how much you can write within a week, and thus help you adjust so that you can achieve your goal of writing and publishing your book in just 90 days.

But remember these are just guidelines. If you are writing a fiction book, it'll obviously take you longer to write, or you may write a collection of poems, which is shorter, yet inspiration may come at various times throughout your week. You can also choose to write a lot one week, and less the next. Or you may find that one week you don't have time to write at all and then you make up for it by spending four hours, instead of two writing the following week.

It's all totally up to you, and the goal is to have a plan, yet to stay flexible. The more you know what kind of writing routine you enjoy most or works best for you, the easier it will be for your to write your book and achieve your goal.

In this book, I am taking you through 12 specific steps I use with my clients, but of course you are welcome to adapt them in any way you see fit for your personal use.

Have a deadline

So again, if you follow this guide as you write your own, you will see that we allocate about four weeks or four steps for the writing process as there are quite a few other things such as the editing part, or the designing of the book as well as the publishing and marketing processes to take into account if we want your book to be out and available for sales in just three months!

The next most important thing as part of the planning stage is that you take all of these steps into account and come up with a deadline that suits you best.

By now you must have in mind a date that you plan to have your book published. It should be 90 days after you've begun Step 1.

Having someone who can hold you accountable is crucial at this stage.

If you don't have a personal coach, then I suggest that you:

Tell at least two friends that you trust about your deadline - your release date! They need to be people whom you know will support you, will encourage you, push you but just enough to keep you motivated (and not pester you about how much you've written or how far along you've come every single day). Just ask them to check on your every week or every month to see how far you've come.

Create an alarm on your phone that will remind you when your "writing time" is. I also suggest having an alarm on a specific time every week to re-read the chapter on the step you're supposed to be at and work on that during that particular week!

Write down in your calendar when you plan for your book to be published and available online - write down a date and a time!

Choose a pre-launch date (about a week before you officially publish your book) and add that to your calendar too!

When I work with my clients, we announce the release date of the book to the world once the first draft of the book is finished. Now, you don't have to do this. I'd suggest you do this only if you know that your sense of duty will be stronger - you hate to disappoint people so by telling everyone on social media for example, that you're publishing a book on that particular day, you know you'll make it happen one way or another!

However, if you tend to procrastinate a lot, or if this causes you to feel anxious or stressed, then don't do that. Again, do what feels right, but do what you know you'll need to do to make your dream come true! Remember? That's what you chose a little while back!

Set up your sacred space

Part of the planning process also includes setting up a special "office" or a place just for yourself, which you love and where you feel really comfortable writing.

You can set up some candles, soothing decorations, be surrounded by books or even take your laptop in a secluded corner of the garden if that's where you feel most inspired to be as you write your book.

This is a very personal thing, and you should do whatever feels right for you.

Also, make sure that you gently explain to your partner and family members (yes, even to your children, no matter how young they are) at this stage, that you will be spending some time over the next few weeks writing a book, and ask that they respect that by not disturbing you unless there is an emergency of course.

When you are writing, turn off all electronic devices. If you have WIFI on your phone, turn it off while you write. It seems obvious but we don't do it enough. Multi-tasking doesn't work and you have to focus when you write.

Then, once you have a clear idea of when you'll publish your book, and have a sacred space and some time set up just for that, you can rub your hands together and get super excited, as you are now fully entering the "Writing phase".

Step 4: Imagine

You may find that these next few chapters are slightly shorter and lighter, but that's because they are meant to help you stay focused and motivated as you write, all while not disturbing you as you write. You must focus on the flow of your writing, no matter what may be going on outside.

When I work with my clients, I incorporate a lot of elements and use various techniques to boost their creativity and this fifth week is all about teaching them how to harness the power of their imagination to then use it to boost their creativity and help them make our dream to write and publish our book come true.

We use it using frequencies, obviously, and I take them on Quantum Journeys, which are some kind of meditations that help unlock their hidden gifts and talents.

But there are a few ways you can develop the power of your imagination on your own too.

Imagination, in my opinion, is our very special gift and our super-power in a way. It is the one thing we all have and that allows us to create anything we want and then to "bring it into existence".

Just like Einstein said: "Logic takes you from A to B. Imagination takes you everywhere".

Imagination encircles the world. Truly!

Look around you. Everything that you're surrounded with first existed only as an idea in someone's mind.

The computer you're using, the bed you're lying on, the chair you're sitting on, the plane you're travelling on to get to other countries, the car you're using to get to work, the shoes you're putting on every day to protect your feet!

Everything was created by someone who first thought about it, and then shared his or her idea or worked on it themselves and, quite literally, created it so that it now exists in our world today!

So our imagination is no small thing. I believe we seriously take it for granted. Everyone does. I believe it is something young children revel in but that (many) adults fear.

Our society condemns imagination. Think about it! Children with an over-active imagination are told to conform, to stop dreaming and rather, to focus on what's "real". We feel almost like fools when we talk to our friends, colleagues and even family members about those big dreams that we have. As we get older, we discard our imagination as something childish and unrealistic.

When in fact the opposite is true! Look at all of the movies that come out every year. How many people have enjoyed Game of Thrones? Harry Potter? The Lord of the Ring? Dune? Millions if not billions!

Look at all of the books that are being published every year. What are the most popular genres?

According to an article published in 2020 by theproactivewriter.com, "the best-selling book genre is romance and the most profitable fiction book genre. Religious and inspirational books are the most popular non-fiction genre, whilst thrillers are the most popular audiobooks."

What does that tell you? Imagination is still very much alive. People don't just love it, they crave it! Imagination is the fabric of our world. It is both what makes the world, it is also what makes us. On top of that, it is also what allows us to create in the world.

It is pretty much a "multi-dimensional portal" to the creative doorways of our minds. Think about self-help books. They too have been written by imaginative men and women who have gone through something important in their lives and have come up with creative solutions to various issues, problems or challenges.

Biographies, even though they may be "realistic" accounts of a person's life, are, to the readers, stories that they identify with. They may not have lived the same lives but may have gone through similar or even identical experiences. How do they empathise and identify with another person? They put themselves in other people's shoes by using their imagination!

Imagination is everything! And so when you write your book, no matter what it is you decide to write about, I highly recommend that you forget about whatever you've been taught about what's possible or not, what's real or not, and allow your imagination to run free!

See where it takes you!

On an energetic level, imagination is also very, very important. Did you know that your brain cannot differentiate between what is "real" and what is not?

This means that if you think now about a moment in the past when you were in danger, adrenaline will start to rush through your body because the brain will think you're in danger right now. In the same way, if you imagine a dangerous situation that "may" occur in the future, the same thing will happen, even if it never actually happens.

Unfortunately, this is how most of us, humans, use our imagination these days; we think about what may go wrong, which triggers our freeze, fight or flight response and leaves us constantly stressed and drained!

This has terrible implications because, for one, we make our bodies sick, as whatever we think about past, present, future, imagined or not affects our physiology and, secondly, as vibrational beings, doing so leads us to emit lower frequencies, which means that we, in turn, attract people, situations and circumstances in our lives which also emit lower vibrations.

The wonderful thing here, however, is that by using our imagination, we can also reverse all that.

We can literally train our brain to imagine the best outcomes to all situations that we wish and, as a result, become healthier and happier.

And guess what? When we do that, it turns out we attract more good people, things, situations in our lives and, yes, that also means that we have a much higher chance to make our dreams come true!

In a way, we work in sync with the Universe, or God, when we use our imagination.

And using your imagination for your own benefit is non-negotiable!

So, from today, I want you to apply the 15-15-15 rule.

15 minutes visualising in the morning, during the day, and right before sleep.

I want you to visualise or imagine as vividly as you can, anything that has to do with your book and enjoy the feeling:

What are you wearing?

Where are you?

Who are you with?

Look at your book which you have in your hands, what does it look like?

Hold it against your chest, how does that feel?

You are browsing books on Amazon and you see your book is listed amongst the best-sellers, how exhilarated do you feel?

Have fun and play around with as many images as possible. Add sounds (people cheering you on), sensations (your loved ones hugging you as they congratulation you on your achievement), smells (any book lover knows how new books smell, I couldn't wait to smell mine! How does yours smell as you open the package and breathe in the smell of freshly printed ink?) etc.

And then either re-live the same scenario every day or try and keep it as consistent as possible.

Personal Tip: Even better, take a "snapshot" of what it means to experience the successful feeling of having your book published.

Is it looking at a photo of you beaming while crushing your book against your chest?

How did you feel when the picture was taken (in your imagination)?

How does it make you feel every time you see that picture and re-live the moment (that happened in your imagination).

Don't worry if the cover of the book changes in your "visions", just focus on experiencing the same exhilarated feeling for 15 minutes, three times a day: as you wake up, during your lunch break or as you meditate, and at night before you fall asleep.

Do this consistently over the next few weeks, and believe me, you will not only achieve your goal to write and publish your amazing book in just 90 days, but all sorts of miracles will also happen all around you!

Step 5: Write

Now that you have all the tools you need, your task is to focus on your writing. Make it as enjoyable, as fun and as fulfilling as possible.

Don't rush to the end, enjoy the process. Enjoy the journey.

Also, don't stay stuck in one place. Avoid rereading your manuscript from the first chapter every time you open your Word document because you may never get to the end.

I must have read and reworked the first chapter of my book Izel, the Black Panther at least 100 times over the last 10 years. I'm not even joking!

The worst part was that in 2014, when I reviewed it and had managed to edit half of the entire book, and I switched computers, my mother lost the USB drive on which I had saved the updated version of my book. I lost it all and needless to say that it put me off reviewing it again for years.

Then in 2020, I managed to find an older version of the manuscript and had to review it from scratch once again. In the end, it was almost meant to be, as I like the story a lot more now, but still, it was a good reminder to always save my document several times in several places, and that spending ages reviewing the first few paragraphs over and over again is pointless.

A book will never be perfect, or, should I say, can always be improved! There are dozens of ways to say one thing or to describe a place. But as long as you're satisfied with it, keep moving forward.

This week, simply take a deep breath and dive into your writing. Don't even correct spelling or grammar mistakes (that way you know you will have to go back and re-check the entire manuscript once the first draft is over) but for now, just focus on writing that first draft, completing it, reaching the end of your story or at least writing down all of your ideas even if you need to re-organise them later.

The most important thing here is to allow your thoughts to flow without being too rigid with the structure of your book, or even with the outcome.

Don't worry too much if what you write makes sense or not, and allow your words to come from your heart, and not from your mind, if you see what I mean.

That way, they will flow more naturally, and as a result, your book will seem a lot more fluid, but also more genuine and a lot more interesting to your ideal readers.

The more you try to have a perfect first draft, the more you will likely lose in quality over time as you may lose track of what you're trying to say or write about because you're too focused on the details.

So write, write, write. One very cool technique that I use before I begin to write is to clear my head by visualising inspiring a beautiful bright silver light and, as it enters through my nostrils, I picture that light cleansing and brightening each part of my head, body, and every cell.

As I exhale, slightly darker silver light comes out of my mouth or nose. I then repeat the process until I visualise pure silver light both enter and come out of my nose. Because you focus on your breathing as you do this, it'll allow you to clear your thoughts and because you visualise something vividly, it'll boost your creative powers instantly.

You can also try the 4-4-4-4 breathing technique which can also help you focus on the task at hand, right before you start writing. Simply look at a square picture frame or shape in front of you and inhale for four seconds, then hold for four seconds, exhale for four seconds and hold for four seconds. Repeat three times.

You might get a little dizzy at first, but with practice, it'll get easier. I suggest you do this three times a day. It'll help you re-centre, especially if you find your thoughts are floating around as you write and you find yourself being distracted.

Step 6: Focus

Our ability to set intentions, get clear on a goal or goals and then to take inspired, conscious actions that lead us in the direction of what we want to be, do or have, are some of the things human beings do very well and they are of course the main ingredients to success.

It is our ability to focus that allows us to turn thoughts into things. When we concentrate, when we put all of our energy into one task at a time, when we stay true to our heart and intent on achieving a particular outcome, we harness tremendous power: the power to create or manifest anything that we want.

I think that we highly underestimate this power and, because we live in a society of consumerism in which we are constantly distracted, most of us have even lost touch with this power.

Yet all of the extremely successful people such as Bill Gates, Steve Jobs, Tony Robbins, Oprah, Abraham Hicks, Elon Musk etc, will tell you that without focus, they wouldn't have gotten to where they are now.

Focus includes consistency, or our ability to carry on and do things even if we don't necessarily feel like doing them, which is closely related to and even intertwined with discipline.

As much as writers should listen to their creative instincts, they also must develop a routine, stay disciplined and focused on what they are creating.

This is why some writers sometimes shut themselves off from the world and other people when they write. The level of concentration that is required to put together a story that makes sense from beginning to end, is tremendous. We may even forget to eat or, like me, simply never get hungry.

I was so focused on my writing that I lost six kilograms in seven months, simply because I was drinking a lot of water (which you should by the way, as it keeps your mind sharp and hydration is essential for your cells and neurons to function properly) and I could write for hours without stopping.

Of course don't write because you want to loose weight! All I'm saying, and it's the case for any kind of activity one is passionate about, is that when you're extremely focused on doing, especially something you love and enjoy, you loose track of time. And that is the power of focus.

However, to be able to focus, all while enjoying a balanced lifestyle, it may help to set up an alarm every day to remind you to open your laptop, just to see if you write anything or not, but at least to get your brain and body used to "getting into the writing mode".

One exercise I love to do, when I don't particularly feel like writing, is to tell myself that I will open my manuscript for just 15 seconds and if I don't feel like writing anything then, I will close it. Interestingly enough, more than 60% of the time, I would always write something.

Writing a little bit at a time is always better than to write nothing at all - unless, of course, you're able to write a whole 50 pages in one single morning, and this works better for you than writing five pages every day.

However, it is important to remain healthy, no matter what you're doing, be it writing or any other activity. Don't forget to take regular breaks, to drink a lot of water, to put time aside to go for a walk, to still enjoy mealtimes with your family or, of you live alone, to set up yet another alarm to remind you to eat something and, when you do, choose to eat healthy food. It's tempting to get a takeaway meal quickly just to be able to go back into your writing, I know, but having been there and done that, it is way more sustainable, and you'll find it easier to write, if you're keeping in shape, and also taking time out and away from your computer screen!

I usually also suggest, as I do with my clients, that they do at least one or two exercises every day that have nothing to do with writing, as it will help you develop your ability to focus without you even realising it.

We are all different so find what works for you but one very efficient way to increase your ability to focus is to take five minutes every day and focus on the light of a candle. You wouldn't believe how powerful this is! Just five minutes of doing this really will do wonders to help increase your concentration. Give it a try!

Of course doing yoga, meditation or breathing deeply helps as well.

Something else that's also important to remember, is that every great writer reads!

Not only will reading help you to instinctively come up with better sentences and will help broaden your vocabulary, but it will also help you concentrate since you are fully in the present moment when you are drawn into a book. Just make sure it is something you truly enjoy reading (don't read for the sake of reading!).

Last but not least, while focusing is good for any writer, just like everything else, being too focused for too long can be bad for you too.

Focusing too much can lead you to take things and life too seriously. But the whole writing process needs to be enjoyable!

Don't forget to enjoy the journey getting to where you want to be. Your book will get published and soon enough you'll hold it in your hands. And it'll feel amazing. But what you'll truly appreciate, even then, is the work and effort you put into getting there.

It is very easy to get carried away and to get into a writing frenzy and it's great to have family members or friends who understand what you're doing but you should only focus on your writing for the amount of time you decided on, and then take a clean break away from it. Spend time with your family, pets and friends and do other things that are enjoyable when not writing.

Writing is extremely taxing for our brain so if you're also working full-time or have children to take care of, it's even more important to pace yourself.

Simply have a nice writing routine that makes you feel good both about writing and about your life in general!

Step 7: Flow

Of course, there is no right or wrong way to write a book. Every book is different, just like everyone is different.

Yes there are writing schools, that'll help you be a better writer, and some are more naturally skilled in the use of words than others, but I believe anyone can write a book, and then work with it in a way that's best for them, whether it involves hiring someone to help them edit their manuscript or design their cover for instance.

What's important is to always trust your instincts. And that's personally what I love most about writing and self-publishing. We are free to do whatever we want.

It doesn't mean however that it is never hard. Writing a book is not easy. Mostly because as a writer you want to make sure you write what you consider a "great" book".

By now you should have completed about 80% of your manuscript if writing and publishing your book in 90 days is still your goal.

There will be times when writing will come to you much more easily and other times when the words won't come. This may be because old fears are resurfacing. Are you good enough to write? Can you actually do this? Or because you begin to get tired, you may even get annoyed at your own characters, or you may not enjoy your writing routine anymore.

I think every writer reaches a moment when they're almost willing to give up. And to me, this is absolutely normal and, in a way, it is a test. Many people have dreams, but only a few make them true.

Why do you think that is? Many people stop when the going gets tough. It's the truth.

Because it felt exciting to write at the beginning, words flowed to you easily and it was all something you thoroughly enjoyed doing.

But somewhere along the way, life may have got in the way. Unpredictable things happen, and although you've proudly stuck with your writing routine for a good three to four weeks, you feel less enthusiastic about this now.

That's also absolutely fine. And it just means that you need to get back in the flow as naturally as possible.

I'd like to use a metaphor here.

Just imagine yourself on a little boat that is floating down a river.

You are going with the flow (your writing comes to you easily), the journey is enjoyable and relaxing.

Then, once in a while, you arrive at various checkpoints, where they give you water, food and you can take some pictures.

This is when you take a bit of time to assess how far you have come. It's actually very important to appreciate what you've accomplished already and celebrate the small wins!

Every chapter you've written is a milestone. It's a victory! It's taking you one step closer to making your dream to publish your first book come true!

But don't dilly dally there either. Once you've enjoyed the view, remember that you're in for a fun ride, get back in the boat with a broad smile on your face, and keep going.

You then soon find that there are times when the water gets rougher, the currents get stronger, or when your boat gets stuck in between rocks. It may even get dragged to the side on a sandbank and you have to get out and pull it back into the water.

The same may be happening with your writing. Perhaps you don't feel confident you're getting anywhere, or you are doubting your ability to finish your book.

Doubts start to pile up and after a while, you begin to lack motivation, you don't feel inspired anymore. You lack energy or, simply, you just have no clue where to go from there.

So you start to do other things, you forget about your book for a while, you tell yourself you can do it later, after all, you don't have to do it now.

True, you don't! But if not now, then when? Yes, maybe it is not the right time for you. That's possible, and in that case, you'll know because you'll just not feel any desire to keep on writing.

If that happens to you, save your manuscript and keep it somewhere safe. You'll go back to it in the end - even if it takes you ten years to do so!

But if you feel guilty because you know you should be writing, as this is what you want deep down, you may come up with tons of excuses as to why you can't write (you might even get physically sick, or begin to develop migraines when on the computer for example), but you are, quite simply, procrastinating.

And that's fine too!

I believe procrastinating is good, at least for a while.

Most people procrastinate when irrational fears start to emerge. We suddenly (or in general for some people) feel that we are not good enough and can't live up to our own, or others', expectations.

Usually, when we are asked to help someone else, even if we don't feel like doing it, it is harder to back down if we've agreed to help because there is another person involved, and we don't want to hurt their feelings, for example.

But when we are all alone, achieving the goals we set up for ourselves is an inside job. And we can be our biggest supporter or our worst enemy.

So, when you begin to feel very guilty or annoyed because you know you should be writing and you can't bring yourself to do it or you keep putting it off, the first thing to do is to become fully aware of what's happening.

Realise that you are indeed procrastinating and simply accept it.

You can explore why you may be feeling that way, but more often than not, this might result in you finding yet more reasons or excuses for you to be afraid of the next step.

Try not to be in denial by acknowledging the fact that you have some fears and doubts and are not sure you can do this.

Also acknowledge that feeling inside of you that knows that you want to achieve that particular goal because if you didn't, you wouldn't be feeling so uncomfortable about it. You simply wouldn't care.

But you do, right? And that is a good sign!

Then, give yourself a full day or two days (three at most) off! Take a clean break from your writing.

Decide there and then that you will not worry about your manuscript for a few days. Let yourself feel totally happy and guilt-free about that time you're giving yourself.

If you're writing full-time, take a weekend off, go to the beach, do something fun, meet friends for coffee or dinner, go for a long walk, whatever it is that you want. Treat yourself shamelessly. Relax and recharge.

If you're working and/or have a family, focus more on spending more time with your partner and children. If you're living on your own, use the time you were spending in front of your computer to treat yourself. Have a bath, read a good book, watch a TV series, go out with friends, go on mini-holidays etc! Do more things that feel good.

Then, one, two or three (maximum) days later, once that break is over, STILL do NOT think about your writing!

This is very important. Here is what I want you to do:

I want you to wake up that morning, and focus on one thing that feels good to you, whether it's a song, or just focus on not thinking about anything.

If you can't, then choose a word or sentence/mantra such as "I'm feeling so good", "I'm happy" - whatever works for you - and repeat it to yourself again and again. Do this the entire time while you have your breakfast.

Do not wonder if you should go to your computer now or later, simply keep repeating that sentence to yourself, write it down if you must carry it around and read it out loud, but do not think (tough, I know, but just trust me!)!

Then get in front of your computer screen, still not thinking, and open your manuscript.

There, take a deep breath in and out, five times, while repeating the sentence you chose "I'm happy", or "today's fun" (again, it has to be whatever works best for you).

If you are still writing your first draft, go straight to where you last stopped and begin by rereading the last chapter you wrote.

If you have finished your first draft, get ready for the next step; the editing process. Just take your book where you left it.

And here, give yourself five minutes.

Look at the time. Let's say, for example, that it's 8 am. Just tell yourself that you'll look at the time again in five minutes.

If you're like me, once you've begun to read your last chapter or sentence, and start correcting a couple of things or keep on writing, you'll get sucked right back into your work!

You will also quickly feel a wave of relief and pride, because, as hard as it may be to do whatever it is you're doing now, you're doing it!

If you do end up looking at the clock again and it's 8:05 am, just tell yourself, "okay, I'll do this just five more minutes" and carry on until you completely forget to look at the clock.

Give yourself an easy, realistic but slightly challenging and fulfilling goal to achieve that week such as, working on your book fifteen minutes every day or for one hour, two days in a row.

The best thing about doing this is that by the time you reach step 8, you'll be feeling wonderful about having had a much-needed break and about still having been able to accomplish something.

This technique is one of the best ways to beat procrastination and the "writer's block" together.

So, whenever you feel that words are not flowing, or that things are not quite going your way, rather than getting frustrated, allow yourself to take some mini-breaks.

Take a walk, take a shower, call a friend, watch a movie, play a game, change scenery, or you can even have fun writing something else, or spend time imagining your story as a movie playing in your mind.

If nothing helps and words still don't come to you, you could also try and talk into a recorder.

Just imagine you're explaining what your book is about to a friend, and record yourself as you speak.

Let's say you've written 22 chapters and you know you're approaching the end of your book, say out loud how you think the story should be like, what the ending could or should be and why what the readers will love to know or understand and what the overall message of the book is.

This alone might give you some much-needed inspiration. You might even want to use a software like Otter and use it to transcribe what you say out loud into writing and use this to help you finish your first draft!

Another thing you can try is to become totally still. If you're someone who enjoys meditating, then you understand what I'm saying.

Ideas and inspiration really flow when you reach a meditative state. If you don't particularly like meditation, find a frequency or binaural beat on Youtube that you enjoy (you can type anything nowadays from "music to focus" to "focus frequency") and lie down for a while as you listen to it.

Or feel free to get in touch with me and I'll give you the perfect frequency that matches your particular need(s) which you can listen to while you write.

All of these will help you get back into this Flow-like state where words, ideas will once again naturally come to you.

Step 8: Edit

Well, congratulations! You should have by now completed your first draft! This is no small feat so do celebrate yourself right now! You deserve it! You've written an entire book all on your own!

YOUR FIRST BOOK!

Now it's time for you to go back to the very beginning of your amazing story, and edit your manuscript!

If you follow the steps I outline in this chapter, you will be able to properly and thoroughly review and edit your entire book in just one week!

I was able to develop this technique or process both thanks to my background in journalism as I have worked for many years first as an editorial assistant and then as the owner and editor of my own magazines (Wildlife Geographic and

Luangwa Wildlife Magazine), and because I edited the nine books I published on Amazon myself (both in English and French).

It works really well for pretty much any type of book and is hugely popular with all of my clients. Of course, you may still hire a professional editor or proofreader. I, myself, proofread my clients' books as part of my programme.

However, it is also entirely possible to edit your own book as long as you follow all of the following steps carefully.

Remember that all of these steps should be completed in *one week* or two weeks for fiction/fantasy/thriller writers at most.

Step 1 (day 1)

Start at the beginning of your manuscript and simply by scrolling through the entire book looking for spelling/typing mistakes and correcting them as you go - these are the words in your Word document that will have that red line underneath them.

Here is an example:

> I was able to develop this tech.nique or process both thanks to my background in journalism as I have worked for many years first as an editorial assistant and then as the owner and editor of my own magazines (Wildlife Geographic and Luangwa Wildlife Magazine), and because I edited the nine books I published on Amazon myself (both in English and French).

Some underlined words might be names of people or places, which you should still re-read to make sure they're spelled correctly, but then you can ignore those.

This is a great way to start the editing process, because you don't need to read anything here. You just need to scroll down and correct those underlined words.

Step 2 (day 2 and 3)

Next, go back to the beginning of your manuscript again and, this time, re-read everything. This is the most difficult and most important part of the editing process.

Take your time! I'd suggest taking at least three days to focus on just this part of the process.

As you go through your book, read every single sentence. Add missing words, reword sentences that can be reworded.

Also, try to read it "from the reader's perspective" and ask yourself:

Is everything making sense?

Is everything I wanted to express here? Have I forgotten anything?

Is the timeline correct?

Does it flow?

Does it sound fun or boring?

Did I incorporate the right amount of dialogue?

How do I feel about the book overall?

Is there anything I can change/ add to make this paragraph better?

Be very careful with this process so that you don't need to do the same thorough check twice. Focus on doing it properly.

It will take you a little while, but it's worth it! This is where you get to polish your manuscript.

As an editor, I realised that for most people, be it my fellow authors, or my staff writers, the second draft is usually the best, so do not underestimate the importance of this step. Even if it takes you longer than you think.

Step 3 (day 4)

Then, once you've edited your manuscript yourself, properly, nicely and you are confident you did a great job, run it through Grammarly.

Grammarly is a free online app/software which you can install on Safari or Google Chrome and use anywhere. Even the free version will help you spot mistakes you will have missed.

The paid version also checks for syntax mistakes and gives you more corrections and suggestions, so even though you have to pay for it, it'll still be a lot cheaper than hiring an editor.

Of course, there are other spelling checking softwares available on the market, or you may even want to hire someone on Upwork to review your manuscript, it is up to you but, in my opinion, Grammarly is a great option at this stage.

It will find things that are easy to overlook when you're "too close" to your manuscript such as words written twice next to each other, punctuation mistakes, and other spelling and grammar mistakes you and even Word may have missed.

Step 4 (day 5)

Next, you should go through your book once more! Yep, once more (on average you should be re-reading your book at least 5 times for maximum result, and even so there may still be mistakes!).

Now, one incredibly helpful and efficient, yet very tiring way, to spot mistakes is to carefully read your manuscript out loud.

It takes time, especially if your book is between 150 and 200 pages, but it is an excellent method that'll also help you get a feel of whether your book flows well or not.

I highly recommend you do this especially if you're editing your book totally on your own, that is if you know that you won't be able to find beta readers or people that can read your manuscript before it gets published (more on that later).

Step 5 (day 6)

Then at this stage, take a break!

This is where you step away from your manuscript! Relax and enjoy!

The next step is the last and, ideally, should be completed on the last day of that week.

Step 6 (day 7)

You're almost done with the self-editing process!

This is where you read your book once more, but more as if you'd bought it from a store.

Try not to think of yourself as the writer or author. Don't think about your ideal reader either.

Just be yourself and imagine that you pick up that book in the bookstore and choose to read it. Ask yourself:

Does it flow easily?

Is it interesting?

Do I understand what the book is about?

Do I actually like it?

Personal Tip: Remember that most of us tend to be perfectionists. Again, there is no such thing as a "complete" manuscript. All books can be changed and improved over time.

So just listen to your inner self; you should at the very least be feeling very proud of what you've achieved and know that you have done your very best.

You should be confident that your ideal readers will find and will love your book!

Step 9: Feedback

As I mentioned earlier in the book, having someone genuinely interested in my work, who pushed me beyond my perceived limits, who always encouraged me and believed in me even when I didn't believe in myself was the catalyst that allowed me to write and publish no less than nine books in seven months.

Publishing your first book in 90 days is an extraordinary accomplishment and, if you haven't got a coach to help you through the entire process, I am hoping that this book will be the perfect companion that will help you achieve that goal.

Of course, should you want to work with me privately, I am very happy to coach you through the entire process and I can certainly guarantee that you will write and publish your book in 90 days!

You're also welcome to contact me at any stage of your writing and publishing process, should you have some questions or need some guidance.

I always offer free one-hour complimentary coaching sessions so don't hesitate! Also, as part of my one on one programme, I offer my clients honest feedback on their manuscripts.

Feedback is very important, as it allows you to get a sense of what other people think about your book before it gets published.

In my personal experience, other readers will rarely hate a book that you sincerely enjoyed writing and believe is great work, however, it is important to be open to criticism, and to be ready to adjust or change your manuscript if and when necessary.

Of course, no matter what other people think, the ultimate decision is yours. Whatever changes you make, it is all up to you (as long as you self-publish of course). But it is important to at least be curious about what others think.

Now, at this point, your book should pretty much be ready to publish (even if you haven't designed your cover yet).

But before we get to that, you need to find at least one person, ideally two, that would be willing to read your book, fairly quickly (within a couple of days is best, so choose people you can rely on) and give you their honest feedback.

These can be friends, family members or beta readers. Upwork offers some excellent Beta reading services as well.

Your main goal this week is to see if you have managed to write a story in a way that appeals to your ideal audience if your message or mission or personal transformation is clear enough, or, if your book is meant to be a guide, if it includes practical information your readers find useful and, overall, how good it is.

How much did those people like your book? Did they tell you they loved it so much they couldn't put it down? Do they think other readers enjoy it? Once again, what you do with that feedback is then entirely up to you.

As much as getting people's opinions is important, it's also good to not ask the opinion of too many people because you might feel overwhelmed.

Also, should they have comments or suggestions, it's nice to be able to apply (or not) those changes one manuscript after another.

Also, stay mindful of who the feedback is coming from. Sometimes, even if they have our best interests at heart, our friends or loved ones might not dare be honest enough, because they are don't want to hurt our feelings, or, on the contrary, they might actually be too blunt.

Again, just follow your gut feeling. Always thank them for their time, advice and feedback. If you pay for a professional Beta-reader, remember that it's not because you pay for their services that you'll get good feedback from them, and it's not because they are professionals that you must apply the changes they suggest!

Writing, just like art, is very subjective. So do what you must to publish the best manuscript you possibly can, but, ultimately, do what feels right to you and for your readers!

Step 10: Design

Don't you think we are lucky today to have access to the technology to do almost anything we want on our own?

You don't need to be a photoshop or InDesign expert anymore to be able to design your book cover! While both are fantastic options if you have them and do know how to use them, nowadays there are other, very easy-to-use and affordable platforms which you can use to create your dream cover!

Of course, I am thinking about Canva! I may be biased, but in my opinion, Canva is one of the best tools ever created to help people from all walks of life not just create Social media ads and posts (which will be useful for Step 12), but to do almost anything we want, including making our very own, high-quality book covers!

When I first launched myself as an author I was using the free version of Canva, and that was more than enough for me to play around with dozens of different book cover designs and ultimately decide on the ones I'd use for my various books?

All you need to do is to head to www.canva.com and create a free account. Then simply type "book cover" in the "search" engine and you'll find various templates.

You can select a template you like, or start from scratch. Canva has hundreds of examples, styles, colour palettes, and so much more you can choose from. I highly recommend that you spend this week playing around with it and enjoying the process!

After all, a book cover is very important as it is going to be one of your strongest marketing tools! It needs to be visually attractive to your readers and it will help you build your brand as an author.

You need to make sure your book cover includes your book title (make sure it is quick to read and easy to remember), your full name (or pen name if you prefer to use one), subtitles (if any) or quotations (optional) and at least one image (in the background or anywhere you'd like on the cover).

When designing your front cover you should make sure that it is clear and visually appealing. Don't overload it with too many messages or pictures, and make sure it evokes the right emotions in your readers.

You're welcome to work on the spine and back covers, although it won't be necessary if you publish your book on Amazon.

But if you wish to do so because you want to save the whole lot as a pdf for instance, and then upload it (but then make sure the measurements of your pdf are right), then remember that the spine should include the book title and your name. You may want to include your logo there as well.

Make sure the typography looks nice and is clear. You should have a sharp contrast between the letters and the background (imagine your book on a shelf, make sure it stands out from the others). The font should be large and, obviously, always write your title and name horizontally.

As for the back cover, it should include a summary of your book, but, if possible, you should also add some information about you and even, if you can some reviews or testimonials.

Back to the front cover, remember: "a picture is worth a thousand words". So as much as you may like your story, your book cover should attract your readers all on its own as well.

It must communicate the key message you are trying to convey. Some useful questions you can ask yourself that might help include:

What message do I want to convey in this cover?

What emotion(s) do I want people to feel when they see it?

Is that cover aimed at my target audience?

What types of covers do my ideal readers like best?

What kind of covers do other books like mine have?

Does it look appealing to the eye?

What makes my book unique or stand out?

Here too, if you want someone else to do the work and come up with the whole cover for you, and you can afford their services, you can find some excellent illustrators and book cover artists on Upwork, topkwork.com or Fiverr.

Once you are happy with your cover, make sure you download it from Canva at the highest resolution possible.

Personal Tip: I download my cover as a high quality "pdf print format" and then I right-click on the pdf once it is on my computer, open it in Preview (on Mac / open as an image on PC) and save it as a jpg or png (chose the best quality).

Step 11: Publish

Now that you've got everything ready, it is time to get begin publishing process! How exciting!

The next thing to do, if you haven't done it already is to create a KDP account (Kindle Direct Publishing) at: kdp.amazon.com

Sign up and set up your account. If you already have an Amazon account, you can use the same email and password you normally use on Amazon to create your author's KDP account. Just make sure you have a *valid* phone number associated with that account because KDP will ask you an OTP or verification code which it will send to your phone every time you try to access your personal account where your bank details etc are stored.

If you have any issue, have changed numbers, don't remember your Amazon account password etc, just create a new Gmail address first and, once that's done, create a new Amazon account using that Gmail address and add the right phone number to your new Amazon account.

It'll take a bit more time, but it might actually be useful to create a new Gmail account if, for example, you're launching your book and plan to start a new business that's aligned with what your book is about or if you want to have a special email address your readers can use to contact you (in which case, don't forget to add it at the end of your manuscript too).

You may of course not want to use Gmail, in which case you can use Hotmail, yahoo, or use your professional email to create a new Amazon account, it's totally up to you!

Once you're in your KDP account (not Amazon's "shopping" website, make sure you're logged into kdp.amazon.com as KDP is your publisher's account in a way), head to "Your Account" in the top right corner of the page. There, you need to make sure all your information (bank details, full address, tax information) are correct.

Enter your name, address, phone number etc correctly. Then go to "Getting Paid" in the left menu and enter the relevant information including your IBAN or bank details and tax information.

Once you're all set up, it may take a little while to confirm your details and activate your account, but you can already begin to upload your manuscripts and create your book.

You'll find four sections in your KDP account. The first one is your BOOKSHELF, where you'll be able to create and see all your books, then you have the REPORTS section where you'll be able to see how many people buy your book and what version of your book they buy.

You then have a COMMUNITY section in which there are plenty of forums that'll answer any questions you may have about KDP and the publishing process, and finally the MARKETING section in which you can create and run ads as well as Kindle Countdown deals and free promotions.

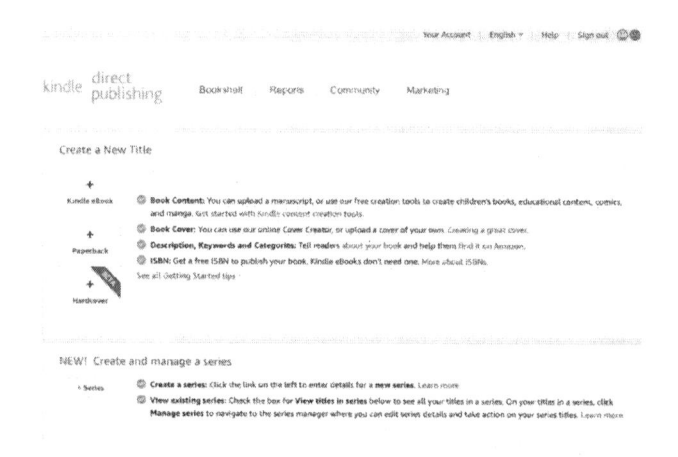

So the first thing to do when your book is finalised.

That means you have your word doc file fully edited, and the high-resolution version of your cover ready to be uploaded - is to go to the BOOKSHELF section.

There, under "Create a New Title", you can choose to create a Kindle book, a Paperback or a Hardcover (new on KDP).

PAPERBACK

I personally recommend that you begin by creating a paperback version of your book. The process here is pretty straightforward.

As you get into "Book Details" (Page 1), you will first be asked to choose the language of your book, to enter the title of the book and subtitle, if any.

Personal Tip: Be careful here. Your book title here and the title written on your book cover must be exactly the same or KDP won't accept your cover. So if you do a book series and write, for example, Book 1 on the book cover, you must also write Book 1 in the title or subtitle section.

Also, note that once your book is published, you'll be able to re-upload a manuscript or change the cover but you'll never be able to change the title of the book ever again - so choose carefully!

You can always un-publish a book and re-upload a new one but doing so means you'd lose all your reviews and ratings so avoid it if you can!

If you want to print a totally updated version of the book and/or cover you'll have to create a new book, but here again, it means you'll lose all previous reviews and ratings.

While you're still in "Book Details" (page 1), you should enter your author's name, the name of the illustrator or of any other contributors and the summary of your book.

You are then asked to choose categories. Make sure you check them all carefully so as to choose the most accurate category possible; the one that suits your book best so that it is ranked as efficiently as possible by Amazon. You can only choose two categories.

Then you need to choose the age of your readers (if they're adults then don't put anything there) and finally, you need to indicate whether your book contains explicit language or not.

When you're done you can head to the next page: "Book Content" (Page 2).

Here you will first be asked if you want Amazon to provide you with a free ISBN.

If you choose yes, remember that you may only publish your book using this ISBN on Amazon.

If you have your own ISBN click no, but if you want to use Amazon's ISBN then click "yes" and then go back to your manuscript (word doc) and copy and paste it after your title and author's name, before your story begins, right above your disclaimer:

This book was published in December 202, by Amazon.com

ISBN :

© Mahina/Maïna Perrot

The moral right of Maïna Perrot to be identified as the authors of this work has been asserted in accordance with the Copyright, Designs and Patents Act, 1988. All rights reserved.

No part of this publication may be reproduced or transmitted in any form or by any means, electronic or mechanical, including photocopy, recording, or any information storage and retrieval system, without permission in writing from the publisher.

It should also be added at the very end of your book, alongside the price of your book, and the publisher's address or website (in this case, amazon.com).

Once that's done you can export your Word or WPS document as a pdf . If you are not sure how to do this, just go to File, at the top left corner of your document, and click on Export to pdf.

Once that's done, come back to your KDP Book Content page. You'll be asked to choose the publication date (you can choose the very day you're putting it on, that's fine), what colours you want inside your book, the size or format of your book (carefully check the one that matches your book here) and whether you want a matt or a glossy cover.

You can also choose your bleed settings but I usually use "no bleed".

Then you can upload your paperback manuscript (Pdf). it'll take a little while and once you're done you can then go to "Launch Cover

Creator" or choose to upload a pdf cover of your book if you have designed one.

Most authors don't design the whole book cover (front, spine and back), but will only have created the front cover so, if that's your case, it's absolutely fine as Cover Creator gives you quite a lot of options.

Once you're in there, play around with the various fonts, colours and layout options KDP offers. Upload your favourite cover on the right page, or front cover, and set it in a way that it looks good.

Then copy and paste the summary of your book at the back and if you want you can add a short biography about yourself. Once you're happy with your cover, click on "preview" and then "save".

When you first create your cover, you won't see the bar-code which Amazon will automatically add for you, so don't worry about it and just know that this is why there is such a big space under your book summary which you can't edit.

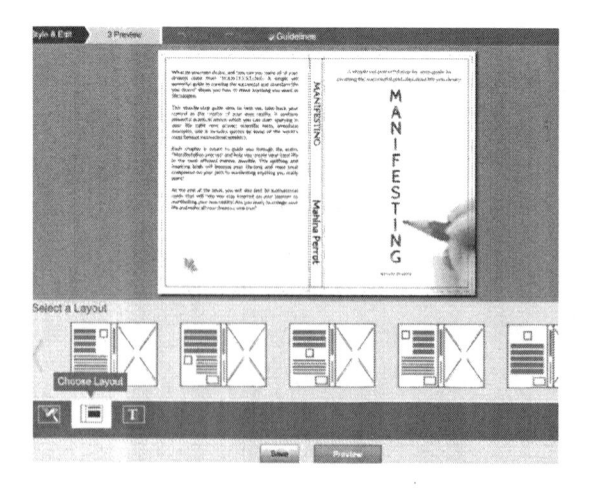

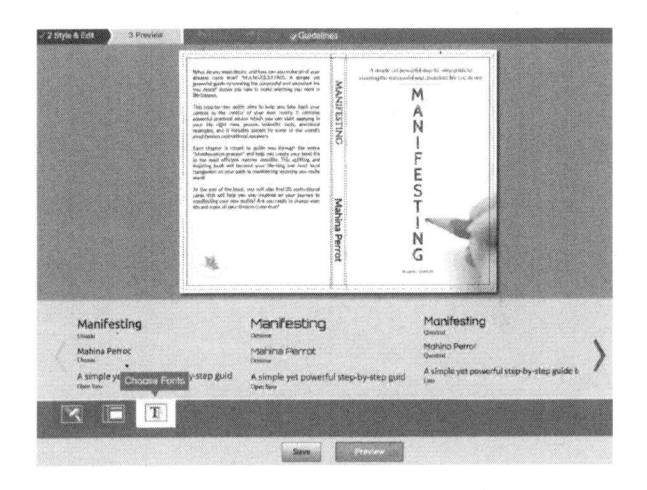

When you are satisfied with your cover, click on "preview" and then "save & submit".

Once you're back on the KDP page, you will be asked to launch Book Previewer. This may take a while, depending on your internet connection quality and speed.

When it is done, however, it will allow you to get a very good look at what your book actually looks like inside and outside, once it is printed. KDP is the only software that, to my knowledge, gives authors such a good and realistic idea of what our book will actually look like.

Most platforms allow you to download pdf files of your cover and book, but, to me, it's not the same. See pictures of what Previewer looks like:

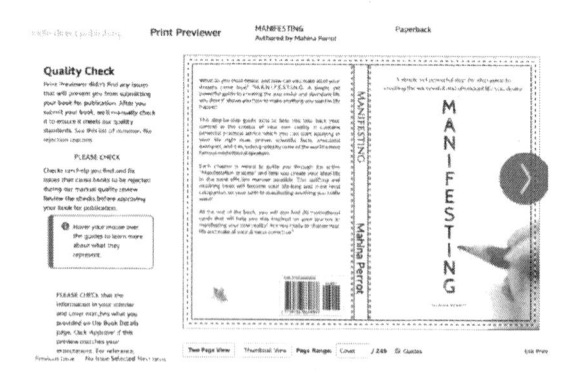

Once that's done, and you have checked all of the pages and are happy with your overall book, click on "approve".

There, Amazon will tell you how much your book costs to print. Again, I've tried various platforms and when you compare the printing costs with the quality of the books Amazon produces, I find that Amazon gives us an excellent deal.

When you're finished, click on "save and continue".

You now get onto "Book Pricing" (Page 3), the last page you'll need to work on before you can officially publish your book!

Here, you will first be asked to choose where your book will be distributed - that is, on which Amazon platforms your book will be available. I recommend choosing "all territories worldwide".

Then you have to select your primary marketplace. You can choose any primary marketplace, but personally, since I have an

Amazon.fr account, I usually choose Amazon.fr and set my book prices in Euros. You may choose to select Amazon.com and set your prices in USD.

Either way, Amazon will instantly show you how much royalty you'll be getting depending on what price you choose for your book.

When you're done, simply select 'publish your book"!

And CONGRATS! You've done it!

Important note! It'll take KDP up to 72 hours (they're usually much faster than that though) to review and approve your book. Just keep that in mind when launching a new book (have your book ready at least a day or two before the official release date!)

If there are any issues they'll send you an email. Most issues have to do with the wrong ISBN being uploaded or the cover and titles being different. If you ever need help, KDP help (top right corner of your KDP account) is an easy way to contact them, and the whole team is extremely quick to reply and very helpful!

Once you're done and your book is LIVE, you will be able to find it on Amazon by typing your book title and your name in the search engine.

To promote or share your book, just share the URL of your book!

KINDLE

As soon as you've published your paperback, you can start to create your Kindle version if you like. It will automatically be linked to your paperback, which is yet another of Amazon's greatest features.

The information in the three pages is pretty much the same, but you will not be able to upload a Word document or pdf version here.

You will first need to go back to your manuscript, and while you're there, delete your ISBN as you won't need it for your Kindle version.

Then choose "save as" and save a second copy which you can rename "YOURBOOKNAME Kindle version" which you will keep on your computer Desktop for now.

Then go ahead and open the Kindle Create app (or download it if you haven't done it yet - type download Kindle Create in Google to find it).

Open it and click on "create new", then "choose" your Word document and wait until it is fully uploaded.

Upload your document and check how it looks in Kindle Create. If your book contains pictures make sure you double-check they're all in the right place, or you may have to re-upload them.

You are welcome to play around with it, and you'll see there are many options you can use. I work on many with my clients, but for the purpose of this book, I have created the following process to help you professionally create your own Kindle book as efficiently and quickly as possible:

Creating a Kindle book is a bit time consuming, but it's actually fun to do but once you've learned how to do one book, you'll be able to do all of your other books!

1. Once your document is open, go to the body (left menu) and check if your book was fully uploaded correctly, with each paragraph looking the exact same way as they look in your printed book.

2. If that's the case, you can actually stop there. If you have used images, double-check they are in the right places, and simply add the Title, Acknowledgements, Foreword etc to the document in the "Front matter" and "Back matter" (scroll down the left-hand side menu) and publish!

If nothing looks normal, which might happen, don't panic. Simply delete everything (right-click: delete in the "Body" section).

3. Then what I suggest you do is add each chapter one by one. In this case, go to your Word or WPS Document and copy your first chapter.

4. Then go to the Body part of the Kindle Create software and click on the + and choose "add chapter page".

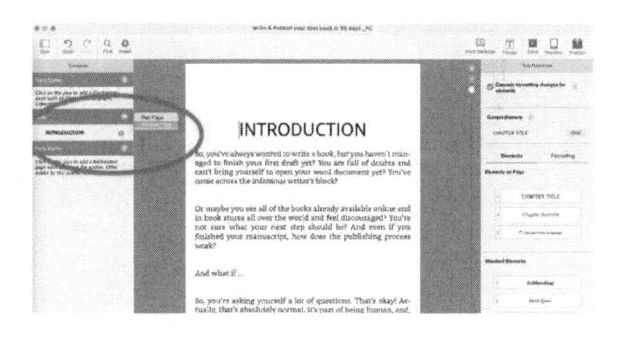

5. Paste your chapter there.

6. Then select your chapter title and, to the right of the software you will see the option "chapter title". Select this.

If you want to change the fonts, go to "formatting" (situated in that same column, next to Elements).

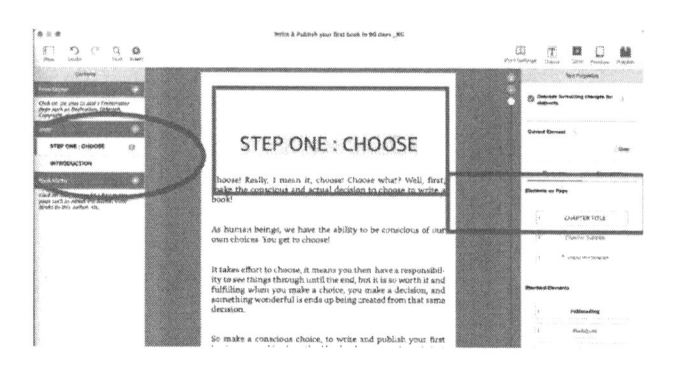

7. Then do the same for each chapter. Don't worry when you see your second chapter appearing before the first one, you can manually change the order of the chapters by dragging the boxes wherever you want.

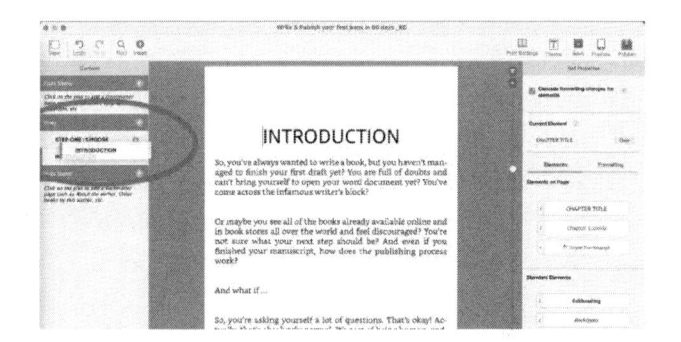

8. Once you have added all your chapters, you can now go to the left menu and click on the little + button next to "Front matter".

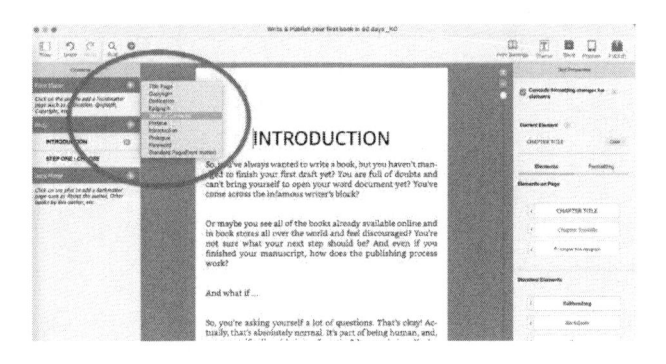

9. Here you can choose whatever you want to add, a preface, a foreword, the title, etc and you can also drag the boxes in the order that you prefer.

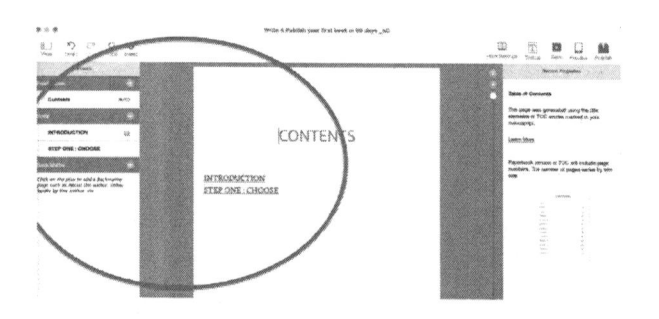

10. Make sure you also select "table of content". This will mean that, once your book is published, all of your chapters are linked to that table of content.

This is great for Kindle readers as they can go straight to the chapter of their choice without having to swipe page after page to get there.

Remember to save your document often, but Kindle Create also reminds you to save your document, which is great.

11. Then, once you've added everything you wanted at the beginning of your book, you can also go to "back matter' (scroll down the Content Menu on the left- and add anything you want, be it an epilogue, an afterword, dedications and thanks etc.

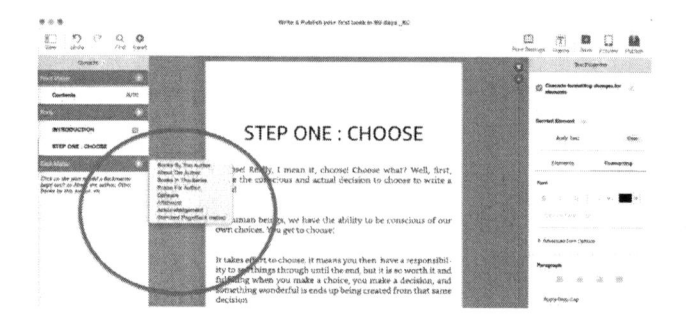

When you're done, click on "publish" in the top right corner and it will save your file as a KPF file, which you will then be able to upload in the "Book Content" (Page 2) section of your Kindle Book which you have started to create on KDP.

Once your Kindle manuscript is uploaded on KDP, you can then Launch Cover Creator again (but here you simply need to add the front cover that you created, no need for the back cover or spine), and once this is done, save and continue until you reach Page 3, choose your pricing and click on the "Publish your book button"

And once again, CONGRATULATIONS! You have now published both a paperback and Kindle version of your book!

Should you want to create a Hardcover, the same process as the paperback applies. Hardcover books are great for fiction or children's books but if you write a biography or a guidebook, you may not need to create it.

Of course, that is also totally up to you. And if you choose to have all three versions available, they'll all be linked together.

That means that when someone buys one of the versions, it doesn't matter which one and they review your book, the review will instantly appear underneath all versions of your book!

Step 12: Market

Woohoo! So, your book is PUBLISHED! That's just brilliant! You've just done what so many people who "say" they'll write a book never actually accomplish.

So give yourself a HUGE pat on the back, open the champagne and, of course, order your author copy of your book!

You can do that from KDP, it'll give you the option to order authors copies (for paperback books only) and although it takes a while for them to arrive, you get to buy them at the price they're being printed! Not the price you're selling your book for!

This is now the last of the 12 weeks you'll have been spending on writing and publishing your book!

You're there already but, as I said at the beginning, publishing your book is the beginning of yet another journey!

Now we want your book to be visible to your readers and reach as many people as possible!

So, what you need to do, once your book is live and available on Amazon, is to create your Author's Profile on Amazon Author Central!

In order to do that, simply go to http://author.amazon.com and create your profile.

Fill up your information correctly, add a little biography and you can even add pictures or videos.

You'll then be able to see any new reviews you get in the Reports + Marketing section of your Author Central account.

Personal Tip: Every time you publish a book or every time you publish your book in a different format (Kindle, paperback, etc) you will need to go to your author's page, and click on the "Books" section at the top, and scroll down until you see the button "add a book".

Just type in the ISBN or the title of your book and once you've found it, click on "add". If you see your book several times, that's fine, but just to be safe, add them all.

Again, if you ever come across any issue, or are confused about anything, check the forums or contact the KDP Help and Amazon Author Central help teams, both of which are both very helpful and responsive.

Setting up your Author's profile is key when you begin to market yourself and your brand as an author.

The next step will be to come up with a marketing strategy. I do this with my clients of course, in order to help them stand out and be seen as leaders in their niche, but here I'll share with you a few things that you can already do on your own to begin to market your book.

One thing that works pretty well is to create and publish book trailers on Social Media. You can either hire someone to do it or do it yourself. There are a lot of people doing book trailers on Fiverr and some are pretty good. You can get a very decent trailer done for about 25$.

Book trailers are an interactive way to present your books to readers because they give them an idea / what your book is about without using any words.

Most trailers use excellent imagery and music and a great designer will be able to convey exactly what your book is all about without even having to read it. Just send them a summary of your book and what you'd like the theme of the trailer to be. A good designer should also be happy to modify your trailer once they've completed it if it is not entirely to your liking, and as long as it doesn't require them to do hours of extra work.

You can also create an author's page, and a variety of posts on Canva, and then promote your books on Social media platforms such as Facebook Instagram, Twitter and Linkedin.

Sharing your posts in various book promotion groups will also be very useful! Just make sure to vary the kind of posts you share! Try and share not just images of your book, but also your own story, your journey, use various images of your book (inside your house, outside, on a fun Canva template etc), and share your trailers and your new reviews!

Go to Goodreads and add yourself as an author there too! Add your books to your profile and begin exchanging with other readers and authors. Ask them to review your book as well!

All social media platforms, including on KDP and Goodreads, give you the possibility to create paid promotions, which will vastly increase your visibility and can help you create an income, but even by doing the promotions yourself, of hiring a virtual assistant to do this for you, you can get a pretty good passive income!

I also found that writing short, appealing posts clearly explaining what the book is about and, above all, what people are going to get out of it work really well.

Just don't forget to always include a link to your book on Amazon so people can purchase it!

Never add the full Amazon link, but shorten it on www.bitly.com for free first. Then copy and paste that new, shortened link in your posts!

Amazon itself helps authors market their books. In the REPORT section of your KDP account, you can see exactly how many books you sell in a month or up to 90 days.

Royalties are usually paid within two to three months but that's the way things normally go with authors. Some platforms even pay authors four months to six months or even a year later so KDP is doing pretty well.

And in the MARKETING section, you can enrol Kindle books only in what is called KDP Select.

Enrolling a book in KDP select means it will potentially reach more readers as your book will be part of the "Kindle Unlimited" bookshelf.

However, it also means that you will be paid by the number of pages read, not per book "sold" since subscribers borrow books and don't buy them. I think you should try and enrol your book in KDP select though because it gives me more options to market it on Amazon.

When you enrol your book in KDP Select it will be for 90 days, which will automatically be renewed unless you cancel it. To cancel the automatic renewal, go back to BOOKSHELF, and click on the three dots (...) next to your Kindle book and choose "KDP Select info".

Why is this important? Because when your book is enrolled in KDP Select it is actually illegal to have it available anywhere else for sales online.

So, for example, you are not allowed to sell an ebook version of your book on your own website during that time.

In short, by enrolling a book in KDP select, you essentially "sign" a contract with Amazon that states that it has exclusivity over your publishing rights for 90 days, so read everything carefully before agreeing to it and then decide whether to keep your book enrolled there or to cancel the enrolment.

I'd still suggest giving it a try first as having your book enrolled in KDP Select has several benefits.

For one, you can run Free Kindle Book Promotions and Kindle Countdown Deals, which allow your books to climb in Amazon's rankings and it's also a fantastic way for you to promote your books as your readers will always appreciate getting a discount.

I normally run a free Kindle promotion either when I would like friends and family members to download the book for free so they can read and review it without having to pay for it, or so that I can get an idea as to how many free books are being downloaded.

This helps give me an idea of the potential number of readers who'd be interested in my book, but who may choose not to pay for it (and that could not just be because of the price of your book, but simply because people prefer to get themselves a muffin with their coffee that day or they think they'll buy it later etc).

Still, when you get 200 downloads every day of your one book every time you run a free Kindle promotion, even though you're not making any profit, it certainly tells you there are people interested in that kind of book out there!

It's also a great way to get reviews. All you need to do when you promote your book as being Free for a couple of days on Kindle, is add a brief or short sentence thanking your readers in advance for reading your book and asking them to take a moment to rank it or review it if they've enjoyed reading it.

KDP also allows you to run Amazon Ads, create A+ Content, and nominate your book for their Kindle Deals and Prime Reading Promotions. You can even enrol in free Amazon Ads Webinar and Amazon Ads training courses, and be a part of the KDP University!

You will also find all you need to know to start your journey as a self-published author right here: https://sell.amazon.com/learn/how-to-sell-books

Of course, you can also decide to get your book reviewed by popular book reviewers. All you need to do is to send them a copy of your books. They are everywhere on Instagram, on Facebook and other platforms.

Personal Tip: To increase your chances to go right up in Amazon's ranking from the very beginning, Get at least 10 friends and family members to buy a copy of your book right as it is launched, say within a day or two of you publishing it for the first time. If they all buy that book the same day, and then five days later, they all review it at the same time, you will climb up the Amazon ladder (which is essentially an algorithm) a lot quicker and thus become more visible.

Conclusion

What's most important though, is that you realise that you've managed to make that one dream come true! Let that sense of achievement shine through every post you make and the Law of Attraction will step in and naturally draw your ideal readers to you!

I deliberately chose to reveal those statistics at the end, not at the beginning of this book, to show you that you've just accomplished something extraordinary!

Did you know that research shows that 97% of people who start to write a book never finish it? Or that out of every 1,000 people that set out to do so, only 30 will complete the task?

Well, YOU have done it! This is incredible and can be proud of yourself! Truly!

So jump for joy, go out and treat yourself and celebrate! Your future self will be grateful to you for having had the courage to go through with it!

Your book is your story, it is a part of yourself, a doorway to your soul, it is your legacy! It is a symbol of your perseverance.

Every time you see it, it will remind you that if you were able to do this, you can accomplish anything!

It is also the real proof that you can make ideas exist, that you can create reality, that you are a creator! You've just added yet another piece of you into this 3D reality.

And everyone who reads that book of yours will benefit from it! They will receive some of your light. Some people will enjoy it, others will be truly moved and/or even changed by it!

Like I always say, "do not underestimate the power of a great book"! So do not underestimate the power of your book!

Also, if you're reading this book and haven't started writing your own yet, it is absolutely fine! There is no better time than now to begin something new!

And it is NEVER too late to turn many more of your other dreams into reality!

Thank you

THANK YOU!

I sincerely hope you enjoyed reading this book and that it will help you write and publish your very own!

If you have a moment and can leave a little review, I would be so very grateful!

If you have any questions, or if you would like to get in touch, feel free to get in touch with me at any time at: mahinaperrotcoach@gmail.com

About the author

Mahina Perrot is a Quantum Manifestation and Writing + Mindset Coach, a self-published author, and former journalist and magazine editor, as well as the owner of ImaginAdventures.

Mahina has a background in communications, psychology and neuroscience and is a Law of Attraction expert and she is passionate about helping other people make their dreams come true. She does so via 1:1 mentoring sessions, through her various coaching programmes and via her various books and weekly Podcasts (available on Youtube/Spotify).

Mahina is also the founder of the 12-week Quantum Writer programme which she has specifically designed to help people write and publish their first book in just 90 days.

She helps her clients improve their mindsets, remove blockages and achieve their goals by using powerful methods that incorporate a mixture of psychological, scientific and spiritual techniques to allow everyone to unleash their full potential.

Mahina is always available to those who have a dream and want to manifest it. She also offers a FREE 60-min complimentary coaching session to anyone who is ready to take action to transform their lives for the better.

You can book your call right here, at a time that is suitable for you:
https://calendly.com/mahinaperrotcoach/complimentary-coaching-session

ISBN: 9798787292220
This book was printed in January 2022
Legal deposit: January 202

Printed in Poland
by Amazon Fulfillment
Poland Sp. z o.o., Wrocław